Received 5/6/02 from Amana Book
living Streams ministry.

D1765597

Life-Study
of
Joshua
Judges
Ruth

Witness Lee

Living Stream Ministry
Anaheim, California

© 1993 Living Stream Ministry

All rights reserved. No part of this work may be reproduced or transmitted in any form or by any means—graphic, electronic, or mechanical, including photocopying, recording, or information storage and retrieval systems—without written permission from the publisher.

First Edition, December 1993.

ISBN 0-87083-743-5

Published by

Living Stream Ministry
2431 W. La Palma Ave., Anaheim, CA 92801 U.S.A.
P. O. Box 2121, Anaheim, CA 92814 U.S.A.

Printed in the United States of America

01 02 03 04 05 / 11 10 9 8 7 6 5 4 3 2

Joshua

CONTENTS

Judges

CONTENTS

Ruth

CONTENTS

MESSAGE THREE   **RUTH'S EXERCISING**   **PAGE 11**
                              OF HER RIGHT

LIFE-STUDY OF JOSHUA

MESSAGE ONE

AN INTRODUCTORY WORD

Scripture Reading: Josh. 1:1-2; Deut. 34:8-9; John 1:17; Col. 1:12; Eph. 3:8; Rom. 6:3-4a; Col. 2:20-21; Eph. 2:6; 6:12; Josh. 6:22-25; Ruth 4:21; Matt. 1:5

With this message we begin the life-study of Joshua, Judges, and Ruth. My burden in the messages on these three books can be expressed by the following four statements:

1) Joshua led Israel to take the God-promised land that it might become the land of Immanuel (Josh. 1:6; Isa. 8:8).

2) Elimelech swerved from the rest of the good land due to the trial of a punishing famine in the God-given land (Ruth 1:1-2).

3) Ruth, an alienated Moabitess, turned to Bethlehem, the place of the holy birth of Christ, and entered into the realm of the divine economy (Ruth 1:16, 19; Micah 5:2).

4) Boaz married Ruth and produced the royal house of David by Jehovah that Christ might be brought in for the accomplishment of God's economy (Ruth 4:13, 21-22; Matt. 1:1, 5-6, 16).

In studying the histories and prophecies of the Old Testament, we need the full scope, the full view, of the entire Scriptures concerning God's eternal economy for Christ and the church, which consummates in the New Jerusalem. This will render us not only a broader view but also the deeper, intrinsic significance of God's purpose in presenting to us the histories and giving us the prophecies of the Old Testament. The scope, the center, and the intrinsic significance of all the histories and the prophecies of the Old Testament must be Christ and His Body, which will ultimately consummate in the New Jerusalem for God's eternal economy.

For God to accomplish such an eternal economy of His,

He needed to create the heavens for the earth, and the earth for man (Zech. 12:1). God created man in His own image and after His likeness with a spirit for man to contact Him, receive Him, keep Him, and take Him as man's life and content. It was very sad that this man got fallen from God and from God's purpose for His economy.

However, out of fallen humankind God chose a man by the name of Abraham and his descendants and made them a particular people as His dear elect among all the nations (the Gentiles). It took God over four hundred years to produce, constitute, and form such an elect to replace the Adamic race for the fulfilling of His eternal economy. God brought such an elect of His through trials, sufferings, both in Egypt and in the wilderness that they might be trained, disciplined, and qualified to coordinate with Him in taking His promised land for Christ on this earth and in providing the proper persons to bring forth Christ into the human race.

To take possession of God's promised land for Christ and to provide the proper persons to bring forth Christ into the human race are the two major points of the section of the history in the Old Testament in the three books of Joshua, Judges, and Ruth. These two main points, to take the land for Christ and to provide the bona fide ancestors for Christ, are the spirit of the history from Joshua to Ruth. They are the intrinsic significance of this section of the Old Testament history. We have to have a clear vision concerning this. Otherwise, our life-study on these three books will be in vain, just like the studies of so many historians, Bible students, and Scripture teachers, either Jewish or Christian.

If by the Lord's mercy we see such a vision, this section of the history in the Old Testament will benefit us the same as the New Testament does. Such a vision will help us to see that the history of God's people on earth is actually the history of the working God energizing among His chosen people in the Old Testament and even the history of the operating God energizing in His redeemed people and having them energize themselves together with Him for the accomplishment of His eternal economy concerning Christ and His increase, which will consummate in the New Jerusalem.

I hope that through the life-study of these three books we all will see and realize that our living, our daily walk, our schooling, our job, and our business must be a part of God's history in His marvelous and excellent move on the earth today. To be a normal Christian, to be today's overcomers, to answer the Lord's present calling, and to meet the Lord's present need in His recovery, it is altogether not sufficient simply to be a so-called good brother or good sister, attending the church meetings regularly, behaving rightly, and living a life which is somewhat perfect in the eyes of men. We need to be one with God in His history, moving, and energizing in His loving overcomers; that is, we need to be one with God in life, in living, and in our entire doing today on this earth! We need to write God's today's history! We need to march on as one with the energizing God! In Him! With Him! By Him! And for Him! We need to be vital, living, and active! We need to be today's Joshuas and Calebs to take possession of the God-promised land for Christ that we may become His possession. We need to be today's Ruths to turn to God's economy, to enter into the land of Immanuel, and to marry ourselves to Christ that we may bring forth Christ to meet the need of men today. This should be the intrinsic life-study of these three books—Joshua, Judges, and Ruth. The issue of this life-study should be the gaining of the God-promised land for Christ and the bringing forth of the excellent Christ to meet today's need of both God and men.

In light of the foregoing, let us now begin our life-study of the book of Joshua.

I. THE FIRST BOOK OF THE TWELVE BOOKS OF HISTORY

Joshua is the first book of the twelve books of history from Joshua to Esther. The Bible begins with the five books of the law, the books of Moses, and then, starting with Joshua, the Bible continues with the twelve books of history.

II. THE WRITER

The writer of the book of Joshua was Joshua (1:1), whose name means "Jehovah Savior," or "the salvation of Jehovah" (Num. 13:16).

III. THE TIME

The time of the writing of this book was 1451-1426 B.C.

IV. THE PLACE

The place of the writing of the book of Joshua was the plains of Moab (Deut. 34:8-9).

V. THE CONTENT

The content of the book of Joshua is that Joshua led the children of Israel to enter the promised land and to take it, possess it, allot it, and enjoy it. The sequence here is quite significant. First, the children of Israel entered the promised land, and then they possessed it and occupied it. Following this, the land was allotted, apportioned, to each tribe in a particular way. Then they enjoyed the land.

VI. THE TYPES OF CHRIST

In the book of Joshua there are two types of Christ— Joshua and the good land.

A. Joshua

The first type of Christ in this book is Joshua himself. The Greek equivalent of the Hebrew name *Joshua* is *Jesus* (Heb. 4:8; Acts 7:45). Joshua typifies Christ and grace (Christ) replacing the law (Moses—Josh. 1:2a; John 1:17). It was when Moses the lawgiver died that Joshua came in (Deut. 34:8-9) to bring the people into the good land (Josh. 1:6), typifying the Lord Jesus bringing the people of God into rest, into the enjoyment of the all-inclusive Christ.

B. The Good Land

The other type of Christ in the book of Joshua is the good land with all its riches (Deut. 8:7-10) typifying the God-given Christ with all His unsearchable riches (Col. 1:12; Eph. 3:8).

VII. THE TYPES RELATED TO CHRIST

The book of Joshua also reveals two types related to Christ.

A. Israel's Possessing and Enjoying
the Promised Land

The first of the types related to Christ is Israel's possessing and enjoying the promised land. This typifies the believers' practical experience of the riches of the blessings in Christ as revealed in the book of Ephesians.

1. Israel's Crossing of the River Jordan

Israel's crossing of the river Jordan typifies the believers' experience of the death of Christ (Rom. 6:3-4a; Col. 2:20), not the believers' physical death.

2. Israel's Entering into the Good Land

Israel's entering into the good land typifies the believers' experience of taking over the heavenlies, where Satan and his power of darkness are (Eph. 2:6; 6:12), not the believers' going to heaven after their death. This is all related to Israel's possessing and enjoying the good land.

B. The Scarlet Thread
through Which Rahab the Harlot Was Saved

The second type related to Christ is the scarlet thread through which Rahab the harlot was saved (Josh. 2:17-19; 6:17, 22-23, 25; Heb. 11:31; James 2:25). This scarlet thread typifies the blood of Christ by which the believers are redeemed (1 Pet. 1:18-19).

VIII. ISRAEL'S TAKING POSSESSION OF THE GOOD LAND BEING IN THE LINE OF BRINGING FORTH CHRIST

Israel's taking possession of the good land was in the line of bringing forth Christ by gaining two females—Rahab and Ruth. These two women play a crucial part in the bringing in of Christ. Rahab as the mother of Boaz became one of the ancestors of Christ (Josh. 2:1-21; 6:22-25; Matt. 1:5a). Ruth was another ancestor of Christ (Ruth 4:21; Matt. 1:5b). She was the wife of Boaz and the great-grandmother of David. Matthew 1:1 says, "The book of the generation of Jesus Christ, the son of David." Hence, Matthew is linked to Ruth and is the continuation of Ruth concerning the bringing in of Christ.

IX. THE CENTRAL THOUGHT

The central thought of the book of Joshua is that God intended to fulfill the promise concerning the good land that Israel might have a place to carry out God's economy, especially to keep the line of bringing in Christ to the earth through His incarnation in humanity. This book is quite wonderful in this main purpose of Israel's occupying and possessing the good land for the carrying out of God's economy.

X. THE SECTIONS

The book of Joshua has four sections: entering into the good land (chs. 1—5), taking possession of the good land (chs. 6—12), allotting the good land (chs. 13—22), and Joshua's departure (chs. 23—24).

LIFE-STUDY OF JOSHUA

MESSAGE TWO

GOD'S COMMISSION

Scripture Reading: Josh. 1

When I was young, I was taught many things concerning the three books of Joshua, Judges, and Ruth, but I was not told that this section of the history in the Old Testament is in line with God's economy. The Bible presents a full picture of God's economy from His creation of the universe to the consummation of the New Jerusalem. The first two chapters of the Bible are on God's creation with man, created in God's image and according to His likeness, as the center. In the last two chapters we have the new heaven and new earth with the New Jerusalem, the corporate expression and manifestation of the Triune God mingled with His redeemed people for eternity. Many things occur between these two ends, but all are linked to God's economy—mainly concerning Christ and His counterpart, the church. The church as Christ's Body will consummate in the New Jerusalem in the millennium for those believers who become mature and in the new heaven and new earth for all the believers.

In Ezekiel 1 God's economy is likened to a great wheel (vv. 15-21). The hub of this great wheel signifies Christ as the center of God's economy, and the rim signifies Christ's counterpart, the church, which consummates in the New Jerusalem. The many believers as the members of Christ are the spokes of the hub spreading to the rim, to the Body of Christ consummating in the New Jerusalem. This great wheel is not just the economy of God but also the moving of the economy of God. From Genesis 1 until the present, this wheel has been continually moving. The move of God's economy has never stopped, and today this great wheel has reached us. When I moved from mainland China to the island of Taiwan with about three hundred fifty to five hundred others more than forty years ago, there were few Christians on that island who knew what God's economy was. But because of the moving of the great wheel of the divine economy, within five years the number in the churches increased to fifty thousand. Eventually, the Lord, the Motivator, burdened me to come to this country. This also was part of the moving of this great wheel. In every age and in every generation, this great wheel has been moving, and today we all are a part of the move of this great wheel on earth. Sometimes the move of this wheel is quite slow, but at other times it is so fast that we can hardly keep up with it.

According to the record in the Old Testament, God's move, which began in Genesis 1, continued through Genesis, Exodus, Leviticus, Numbers, and Deuteronomy. In chapter one of Joshua, God's move had reached a certain situation. At that time the entire earth was full of idols and demons. In a sense, God had been chased away from the earth, which He had created for Himself, and did not have a way to be the Lord of the earth as well as of the heavens. However, among all the nations and peoples, God had separated Israel, His elect, for the carrying out of His economy. They had nothing to do with any idols or demons. On the contrary, they were occupied with the God of the heavens and the earth. After being formed, constituted, disciplined, trained, and qualified, God's people had come to the plains of Moab where they were waiting to enter into the good land, to take it, and to possess it.

One day, as the people were ready and waiting for God's instruction, God came in to call Joshua and to tell him to take the lead so that he and the children of Israel could enter into the good land and possess it. Joshua took the word from Jehovah and charged the children of Israel to perform God's commission (vv. 1-15). The land-takers had to prepare themselves to move with God in His move. In order to take the good land, they had to enter into a full coordination with God in His move. If the children of Israel had looked at themselves, they would have said that there was no possibility. But their possibility was the unique God, who needed His elect people to cooperate with Him in His move to carry out His economy, in His desire to move in His economy as the great wheel. Here God seemed to be saying, "Israel, My elect, you must know that there is no need for you to do anything. Simply cooperate with Me. I am motivating the wheel to run. You need to be one with Me. Go in to possess the land, and I will slaughter the idol worshippers through you. Without you I cannot do anything."

This is the principle of incarnation. In particular, this is the principle of incarnation for the destruction of the satanic power in its usurpation of the earth. This means that in order for God to regain the earth from the usurping hand of the enemy, we need to be in full cooperation and coordination with Him in the principle of incarnation. We need to be one with God in His heart's desire and in His move on earth. Today God wants to save people, but in order to do this, He needs us to be one with Him according to the principle of incarnation.

I. GOD'S CHARGE, PROMISE, AND ENCOURAGEMENT TO JOSHUA

Verses 1 through 9 are God's charge, promise, and encouragement to Joshua.

A. God's Charge

God's charge (vv. 1-4) was that Joshua should enter into God's promised land. His charge to the land-takers was based upon His ordination, initiation, and choosing. The land-takers needed to sacrifice themselves, deny themselves, give up their own interest and preference in all things, and run the risk of their lives for the carrying out of God's eternal economy.

1. The Good Land Having Been Given to Israel by God

In verse 2 God said to Joshua, "Moses My servant is dead; now then arise and cross over this Jordan, you and all this people, into the land which I am giving to them, to the children of Israel." Here we see that the good land had been given to Israel by God.

2. Israel Still Needing to Take the Good Land

"Every place on which the sole of your foot treads I have

given to you, as I promised Moses" (v. 3). This verse indicates that even though God had given Israel the good land, Israel still needed to take the land. On the one hand, there was God's giving of the good land; on the other hand, there was the cooperation of God's people in rising up to fulfill God's commission to possess the land.

3. The Territory of the Good Land

According to verse 4, the territory of the good land included the south—the wilderness; the north—Lebanon; the east—the Great River, the river Euphrates; and the west—the Great Sea, the Mediterranean.

B. God's Promise

God's promise first was that no man would be able to stand before Joshua all the days of his life (v. 5a). Second, God's promise was that He would be with Joshua and would not fail him or forsake him (v. 5b). In verse 9c God said to Joshua, "Jehovah your God is with you wherever you go."

C. God's Encouragement

In verses 6 through 9 we have God's encouragement to Joshua.

1. To Be Strong and Bold

First, God encouraged Joshua to be strong and to be bold (vv. 6a, 7a, 9a). Joshua was to be bold not in himself but in the moving and operating God.

2. Not to Be Afraid or Dismayed

Next, God encouraged Joshua not to be afraid or dismayed (v. 9b).

3. Saying That Joshua Would Have Success Wherever He Went

Furthermore, God told Joshua that he would have success wherever he went (vv. 7c, 8b).

4. In the Term of Walking in the Word of God

God's encouragement to Joshua was in the term of Joshua's walking in the word of God. Joshua was not to turn away from the law given by Moses "to the right or to the left" (v. 7b). The book of the law was not to depart from his mouth, but he was to muse upon it day and night so that he would be certain to do according to all that was written in it (v. 8a). Joshua was to be occupied with God's word and to let the word occupy him. By being occupied and filled with the word, he would have prosperity and success in taking the good land.

II. JOSHUA'S CHARGE TO THE PEOPLE

Verses 10 through 15 are Joshua's charge to the people to prepare provisions for their entering into the good land within three days.

A. To All the People

In verses 10 and 11 Joshua's charge was to all the people. They were to prepare provisions for themselves, for in three days they would be crossing the Jordan to enter and possess the land which Jehovah their God was giving them to possess.

B. To the Two and a Half Tribes

Joshua's charge in verses 12 through 15 was to the two and a half tribes—to the Reubenites, the Gadites, and the half-tribe of Manasseh. Joshua reminded them of Moses' word, saying that their wives, their little ones, and their livestock would remain in the land which Moses had given them, but that they themselves would cross over in battle array before their brothers and help them until Jehovah had given rest to them. This charge indicates that the possessing and enjoying of God's promised land was a corporate matter among all God's chosen people. The land could not be possessed by an individual nor by a single tribe. Rather, all the elect of God were required to rise up, fight for the land, and gain and possess the land, fighting for one another. Then everyone would be able to enter into his particular portion and be at rest.

III. THE PEOPLE'S RESPONSE TO JOSHUA

Verses 16 through 18 are the people's response to Joshua.

A. Willing to Carry Out Joshua's Charge

The people answered Joshua, saying, "All that you have commanded us we will do, and wherever you send us we will go. As in all things we listened to Moses, so we will listen to you" (vv. 16-17a). This indicates that they were willing to carry out Joshua's charge.

B. Blessing Joshua

The people also blessed Joshua, saying, "Only may Jehovah your God be with you, as He was with Moses" (v. 17b).

C. Encouraging Joshua

Finally, the people responded to Joshua by encouraging him, saying to him, "Be strong and be bold" (v. 18b).

The children of Israel agreed with Joshua in taking God's commission. Their response implied their willingness, their readiness, and their being in one accord not only with Joshua but also with Jehovah their God as expressed by their blessing of Joshua in the name of their God. They were one with the Triune God in the great wheel of His economy for the purpose of gaining the good land.

LIFE-STUDY OF JOSHUA

MESSAGE THREE

SPYING OUT THE LAND

Scripture Reading: Josh. 2

Chapter one of Joshua is on the taking of the good land. What is the intrinsic significance of chapter two? Apparently chapter two is on the spying out of the good land, but this is a natural concept. The real intrinsic significance of chapter two is that God gains the right person to bring forth Christ.

In studying the history and the prophecies in the Old Testament, we need to consider the full scope of the Scriptures concerning God's eternal economy. The Bible begins with God's creation, and it ends with Christ as the hub of the great wheel and with the New Jerusalem as the rim to manifest the Triune God for eternity. God's eternal economy, therefore, consists mainly of two things—Christ and His counterpart for the enlargement, the increase, and the spreading of Christ. This counterpart of Christ will ultimately consummate in the New Jerusalem as the full expression of the Triune God for eternity. The intrinsic significance of the book of Joshua is the taking of the land, which typifies our gaining of Christ, plus the gaining of the proper persons to bring forth Christ that Christ might be spread and increased.

Chapter one of Joshua is concerned with the gaining of Christ, and chapter two, with the spreading of Christ, with the bringing forth of Christ to others. For the gaining of Christ, we need to be today's Joshua, fighting the battle, taking the land, and enjoying Christ as our inheritance. For the spreading of Christ, we need to be today's Rahab. Thus, we need to be both a Joshua and a Rahab.

A number of Bible teachers have pointed out that chapter one of Joshua typifies chapter one of Ephesians. Joshua 1 shows us that everything was ready. Israel had been prepared through God's dealing with them for several hundred years in Egypt and for forty years in the wilderness. Israel had become a corporate Joshua, chosen, called, redeemed, saved, trained, prepared, and qualified by God. There in the plains of Moab they did not have any land or inheritance. They were ready to go on with God as one to take the land of Canaan, which typifies the rich, all-inclusive Christ.

In Ephesians 1, which is typified by Joshua 1, we can see that everything has been finished and completed and that every blessing in Christ is there in the heavenlies, waiting for God's chosen, redeemed, and perfected people to take and enjoy as their inheritance. According to this chapter, we have been chosen by God to partake of His holy nature and we have been predestinated by God to have His life in order to become His sons (vv. 4-5). Furthermore, Christ's redemption has brought us into Christ as the embodiment of the Triune God to be the realm in which and the element by which we can be made God's inheritance (vv. 7, 11). Having been redeemed and having been put into Christ as the realm and the element, we are daily being reconstituted and transformed by this element to be a treasure for God's inheritance. As we take Christ and enjoy Him as our inheritance, we become God's inheritance. In addition, we have the sealing and the pledging of the Spirit (vv. 13-14). The Spirit's sealing is the Spirit's soaking and saturating of us in order to transform us. The Spirit's pledging is the guarantee that God is our inheritance. On the one hand, we are God's inheritance, sealed by His Spirit; on the other hand, God is our inheritance, guaranteed by the pledging of the Spirit.

Ephesians chapter two indicates that in the heavenlies there are different layers. Christ is in the highest layer, the third heaven, to be our everything as our good land. But there is a lower layer of the heavenlies—the air, where Satan as the ruler of the authority of the air is frustrating the people on earth from contacting God and from receiving Christ (v. 2). This is typified by the Canaanites, who were frustrating Israel from entering into the good land.

Ephesians 2 also tells us that we were once dead persons (vv. 1, 5), but then God made us, the chosen Rahabs, the enjoyers of Christ. In Ephesians 1 we see Joshua, the believers in Christ receiving all the blessings in Christ. But in Ephesians 2 we see Rahab, all the sinners who were wicked, evil, and dead. Nevertheless, God can perform His dynamic salvation through the redemption of Christ to save such sinners, to make such Rahabs the enjoyers of Christ.

How could Rahab, a Gentile harlot who had sold herself to sin to the uttermost, become a member of the chosen people of God? How could she receive Christ and then bring forth Christ to others for His increase? There was no other way but through faith. Faith comes from the hearing of the gospel. Today people need to hear the good news concerning what God has done through the incarnation, crucifixion, resurrection, and ascension of Christ. People need to hear that everything has been finished and completed and that the all-inclusive Christ is in the heavens for them to receive. However, Satan and his powers in the air try to frustrate them from receiving Christ. The only way this situation can be overcome is by faith. This was Rahab's experience. She heard what God had done for Israel in Egypt and in the wilderness, and she heard how God had defeated Sihon and Og, two strong kings who were the gate guards of Canaan. She heard the good news, and then she believed in the very God of Israel, wanting to be one among His people.

When the two spies came to Jericho, Rahab contacted them and hid them from those who were seeking them. There must have been a good communication between the spies and Rahab, and through this communication she became harmonious with them for God's economy. When she asked them to deal kindly with her father's house and deliver their lives from death, the spies told her to tie a line of scarlet thread in the window. According to the spies' word, she hung the scarlet thread from her window as a sign for the salvation of herself and her entire household, typifying the household salvation of Christ through His redemption by His blood. This is a strong indication that the history in the book of Joshua is related to God's eternal economy concerning Christ in His salvation through redemption.

Eventually Rahab the harlot became one of the excellent,

prominent ancestors of Christ. This Canaanite woman married Salmon, a leader of the tribe of Judah, and through her union with this Jewish leader she became a part of Israel and brought forth Boaz, the great-grandfather of David. What an honor it is that Rahab's name is included in the genealogy of Christ in Matthew 1! This is a strong sign that the history recorded in Joshua is in line with God's eternal economy concerning Christ.

Let us now consider chapter two of Joshua in more detail.

I. JOSHUA'S SENDING OF THE TWO SPIES

Joshua sent the two spies to spy out the good land, especially Jericho (v. 1a). Joshua's real purpose in sending out the spies was to find Rahab.

II. JEHOVAH'S PROVIDING OF RAHAB THE HARLOT

Verses 1b through 22 are concerned with Jehovah's providing of Rahab the harlot. God provided Joshua for the gaining of the land. However, there was the need of a Gentile female for the spreading of Christ, and for this God provided Rahab the harlot.

A. She Having Believed in the God of Israel

Rahab believed in the God of Israel (vv. 8-11; Heb. 11:31a). She told the spies that she knew that Jehovah had given the land to the people of Israel and that all the inhabitants of the land melted before them. She went on to say that they had heard how Jehovah had dried up the water of the Red Sea before Israel when they came out of Egypt and what they did to the two kings of the Amorites, Sihon and Og, whom they utterly destroyed. Then Rahab declared, "Jehovah your God, He is God in heaven above and upon earth beneath" (Josh. 2:11b). Because of her faith in God, she "did not perish with those who were disobedient" (Heb. 11:31a).

B. She Turning to Israel and Their God and Trusting in Him and His People

Rahab turned to Israel and their God, and she trusted in

Him and His people (Josh. 2:12-13). She asked the spies to deal kindly with her father's house and to give her some token of trust that they would preserve her father, mother, brothers, and sisters and deliver their lives from death. She committed herself to them and was pleading with them for mercy. This indicates that she turned her whole being not only to God but also to God's people.

C. She Being Willing to Receive the Spies, Hide Them, and Deliver Them by Her Acts out of Her Faith

Rahab was willing to receive the spies, hide them, and deliver them by her acts out of her faith (vv. 1b-7, 15-16, 22; James 2:25). Her receiving, hiding, and delivering the spies were acts of faith. This indicates that her faith was active. After receiving the spies, she had good fellowship with them concerning what God intended to do.

D. The Sign for Rahab and Her Household to Be Saved

Joshua 2:17-21 speaks of the sign for Rahab and her household to be saved.

1. A Line of Scarlet Thread Hanging in the Window of Her House

The spies told Rahab to hang a line of scarlet thread in the window of her house (v. 18). According to their word, "she tied the scarlet line in the window" (v. 21).

2. Typifying an Open Confession of the Redeeming Blood of Christ

The scarlet thread tied in the window of Rahab's house was hung out in the open; it was there for everyone to see. Thus, the scarlet thread tied to the window typifies an open confession of the redeeming blood of Christ (1 Pet. 1:18-19). Rahab made such an open confession and believed that by this sign she and her household would be delivered.

3. Indicating God's Household Salvation to the Gentile Sinners

This sign for Rahab and her household to be saved indicates God's household salvation to the Gentile sinners (Acts 16:31). We praise the Lord for His marvelous household salvation. Acts 16:30 and 31 reveal that whereas the Lord's salvation is for the individual believer, the unit of His salvation is the household. This is also illustrated by the cases of the whole house of Noah (Gen. 7:1, 13) and of the houses of Israel (Exo. 12:3-4). The case of the whole house of Rahab confirms that the family, the household, is the unit of God's salvation. In the New Testament the principle of household salvation is illustrated by the cases of the house of Zaccheus (Luke 19:5-6, 9), the house of Cornelius (Acts 11:13-14; 10:24, 44, 48), the house of Lydia (16:14-15), and the house of the Philippian jailer (16:32-33).

E. A Condemned Canaanite Qualified to Be Destroyed Becoming One of the Main Ancestors of Christ

Rahab was a condemned Canaanite qualified to be destroyed, but she became one of the main ancestors of Christ, associated with Christ in His incarnation for the fulfillment of God's eternal economy, by turning to God and His people and by being married to Salmon (Matt. 1:5a), the son of a leader of Judah, a leading tribe of Israel (1 Chron. 2:10-11), and probably one of the two spies.

III. THE TWO SPIES' RETURN AND REPORT

Joshua 2 concludes with the two spies' return and report (vv. 23-24). They related to Joshua all that had happened to them and told him that Jehovah had given the land into the hand of Israel and that all the inhabitants of the land had melted before Israel. The report of the spies was a right word in faith, yet Israel still needed to take the land by faith in God, sacrificing themselves for God's interest that they might share in what God had gained for the accomplishment of His eternal economy.

LIFE-STUDY OF JOSHUA

CROSSING THE RIVER JORDAN

Scripture Reading: Josh. 3—4

Chapters three and four are on Israel's crossing of the river Jordan. The people of Israel were ready to enter into the good land and to take it as their possession. However, in their old man they could not gain the victory. Their old man had to be buried so that they could become a new man. This corresponds to the New Testament economy of God. The children of Israel were buried in the death of Christ and then they were resurrected in the resurrection of Christ. This indicates that even in the Old Testament time the children of Israel were identified with Christ and were one with Him. Because they were one with Christ, passing through Christ's experiences, His history became their history. In particular, they passed through Christ's death to bury their old man and to become a new man in Christ for the fighting of the spiritual warfare.

We need to realize that our natural man, our old man, is altogether not qualified to fight the spiritual warfare for the gaining of Christ. God's intention is to join us to Christ to have an organic union between us and Christ, making us one with Christ, that His history might become our history. His history is our story, and our story is His history. We have been identified with Christ to experience what He has gone through. In union with Christ, His experiences become ours. He died on the cross, and we died with Him. He was buried, and we were buried with Him. He was resurrected from the dead, and we were resurrected with Him. Now because we are persons in Christ, we are no longer the old man but the new man.

Let us now consider the various matters related to Israel's crossing the river Jordan.

I. THE ARK OF GOD WITH THE BEARING PRIESTS
TAKING THE LEAD TO GO INTO THE JORDAN
AND STAND STILL IN THE WATERS

The ark of God with the bearing priests took the lead to go into the waters of the Jordan and stood still in the waters (3:3, 6, 8, 11, 14, 17a). The ark was a type of Christ as the embodiment of the Triune God. When the ark of God went with the children of Israel, the Triune God went with them, taking the lead and thus being the first to step into the water. Yet the ark was on the shoulders of the bearing priests. This indicates that the priests bearing the ark became one entity with the Triune God; they were one corporate person. God walked in their walking, and they walked in God's walking. The spread of the Lord's recovery today is through Christ's move together with His bearing priests. We and He walk together as a corporate man.

II. THE FEET OF THE PRIESTS WHO CARRIED THE ARK
DIPPING INTO THE EDGE OF THE WATERS,
AND THE WATERS STANDING AND RISING UP IN A HEAP

When the feet of the priests who carried the ark dipped into the edge of the waters that overflowed all the banks of the Jordan, the waters that flowed down from upstream stood and rose up in a heap a great distance away (vv. 13, 15-16). This was the greatest miracle in human history, and the first miracle performed for Israel as they entered the good land. Such a miracle surely was a sign to the children of Israel that their God was real, true, living, and active.

III. THE PRIESTS WHO CARRIED
THE ARK OF JEHOVAH STANDING
FIRMLY ON DRY GROUND IN THE MIDDLE
OF THE JORDAN UNTIL ALL THE NATION
HAD COMPLETELY CROSSED OVER THE JORDAN

The priests who carried the ark of Jehovah stood firmly on dry ground in the middle of the Jordan, while all Israel was crossing over on dry ground, until all the nation had completely crossed over the Jordan (v. 17; 4:10-11). No doubt it took a long time for about two million people, including children, older ones, and weaker ones, to cross over the river with all the things that they were carrying. However, I believe that the priests were not bothered but, happy about the miracle God had performed, were glad to watch all the people cross over the Jordan.

IV. TWELVE REPRESENTATIVES OF THE TWELVE TRIBES OF ISRAEL TAKING UP TWELVE STONES FROM THE PLACE WHERE THE PRIESTS' FEET STOOD FIRM IN THE MIDDLE OF THE JORDAN AND BRINGING THEM OVER AND LAYING THEM DOWN IN THE PLACE WHERE ISRAEL LODGED THAT NIGHT

Twelve representatives of the twelve tribes of Israel took up twelve stones from the place where the priests' feet stood firm in the middle of the Jordan and brought them over and laid them down in the place where Israel lodged that night (4:1-5, 8). The twelve stones signify the twelve tribes of the new Israel. Their being raised up from the waters of the Jordan signifies resurrection from death. The twelve stones raised up from the water were a sign, signifying that the resurrected new Israel would be a testimony of the crossing of the death water (vv. 6-7, 21-24). This typifies the believers' experience with Christ of the resurrection from death (Rom. 6:3-11).

V. JOSHUA ERECTING TWELVE STONES IN THE MIDDLE OF THE JORDAN, IN THE PLACE WHERE THE FEET OF THE PRIESTS WHO CARRIED THE ARK HAD STOOD

Joshua erected twelve stones in the middle of the Jordan, in the place where the feet of the priests who carried the ark had stood (Josh. 4:9). These were another twelve stones, signifying the twelve tribes of Israel in their old life and in their old nature. Joshua erected these twelve stones in the middle of the Jordan where the ark was, signifying that the Lord wanted Israel in their old nature to remain under the death water of the Jordan. This typifies that the old man of the believers should remain in the death of Christ (Rom. 6:6; Col. 2:20). We who have been identified with Christ in His death and resurrection, who have been resurrected with Christ to become the new man, should leave our old man under His death. We in the church life should all be able to declare that our old man has been buried with Christ and remains under the death of Christ and that we are the new man.

VI. THE PRIESTS WHO CARRIED THE ARK STANDING IN THE MIDDLE OF THE JORDAN UNTIL JOSHUA COMMANDED THEM, ACCORDING TO THE COMMAND OF JEHOVAH, TO COME UP OUT OF THE JORDAN

The priests who carried the ark stood in the middle of the Jordan until all the people had completely crossed over the river and everything was completed and until Joshua commanded them, according to the command of Jehovah, to come up out of the Jordan (Josh. 4:10-11). What a marvelous picture of the move of the Triune God embodied in Christ! As the priests stood in the middle of the Jordan, there was no need for them to be afraid, for the ark was with them. They simply had to look at the ark and be at peace.

The principle is the same with us today. The Triune God is here with us. Because our old man has been buried and our new man is working with the Triune God, we do not need to be troubled by anything that may befall us. The Triune God is with us, and He and we are living together and working together.

VII. THE PRIESTS WHO CARRIED THE ARK COMING UP OUT OF THE MIDDLE OF THE JORDAN, AND THE WATERS OF THE JORDAN RETURNING TO THEIR PLACE

When the priests who carried the ark came up out of the middle of the Jordan, and the soles of the priests' feet were lifted up onto the dry land, the waters of the Jordan returned to their place and went over its banks as before (v. 18).

VIII. THE CROSSING OVER OF THE RIVER JORDAN BEING FOR WAR AGAINST THE SEVEN TRIBES IN CANAAN

The crossing over of the river Jordan was for war against the seven tribes in Canaan (vv. 12-13; 3:10b). As Joshua was participating in this miracle, he was strengthened to take the lead to war against the demonic Canaanites.

IX. JOSHUA ERECTING IN GILGAL
THE TWELVE STONES TAKEN FROM THE JORDAN
AS A MEMORIAL TESTIFYING OF ISRAEL'S CROSSING
OVER THE JORDAN BY JEHOVAH'S MIRACULOUS DEED

After the children of Israel crossed over, Joshua erected in Gilgal the twelve stones taken from the Jordan by the twelve representatives of the twelve tribes, as a memorial testifying of Israel's crossing over the Jordan by Jehovah's miraculous deed (4:20-24).

As we consider Israel's history recorded in Joshua 3 and 4, we need to realize that the same things have happened to us. We died with Christ, we were buried with Him, and we were resurrected with Him to become something new. Ephesians 2 tells us that the believers, who were dead in sin, have been made alive, raised, and seated together with Christ (vv. 5-6) to be one new man (v. 15). This new man is God's masterpiece (v. 10).

LIFE-STUDY OF JOSHUA

MESSAGE FIVE

THE PREPARATION BEFORE THE ATTACK

Scripture Reading: Josh. 5

In this message we will consider chapter five of Joshua. This chapter reveals that all the kings were afraid because of the miraculous crossing of the river Jordan. Before the children of Israel attacked, the Canaanites were already defeated. Their spirit was gone. Although the Israelites had been disciplined, trained, and qualified, after crossing the Jordan they still needed further preparation before the attack.

Joshua 5 covers four matters of intrinsic significance. The first item is circumcision. Circumcision is a continuation of the burial in the death of Christ. By crossing the river Jordan, Israel's old man was buried and they came out to become the new man. This was an objective work done by God. Israel still needed to apply it to their flesh. Therefore, they prepared knives of flint to cut off their foreskins. This cutting was their application of what God had done in the crossing of the river Jordan. By cutting off their flesh to roll away the reproach of Egypt, they were buried and resurrected, both actually and practically.

In the New Testament circumcision means the constant application of the Lord's death to our flesh. Romans 6:3-4 says that we have been baptized into the death of Christ and buried with Him, but Romans 8:13 and Galatians 5:24 tell us that we should apply the circumcision of the cross to our flesh by the Spirit. In fact, our flesh has already been crucified, but in practicality we need to crucify the flesh day by day. This is the reality and practicality of remaining in the death and burial of Christ, and this is the significance of circumcision.

The second item of intrinsic significance in Joshua 5 is the

Passover. The feast of the Passover was held to remember Israel's redemption from the death judgment on the firstborn sons and their salvation from Egypt and from the tyranny of Pharaoh. This is a type of the Lord's table. At the Lord's table we remember Him as the Redeemer and as the Savior. Our portion today is not death but the partaking and enjoying of Christ at His table.

The third item of intrinsic significance is the eating of the produce of the good land. For forty years the children of Israel had been eating manna without any labor on their part. But when the manna ceased, their food could be produced only by cooperating with God. The produce of the land of Canaan came out of farming. This means that it was the result of man's labor and cooperation with God. This is in keeping with Genesis 2:5, which says that God sends the rain and man tills the ground. This refers to the cooperation of man and God.

Both the manna and the produce of the good land typify Christ. Christ in the stage typified by the produce of the good land is different from Christ in the stage typified by manna. John 6, which is not a deep chapter, speaks of Christ as the manna who came down from heaven to feed us. In the Epistles Christ is no longer just manna; He is the produce of the good land, prepared through our laboring cooperation with God. This brings in more Christ for ourselves and others and provides a surplus to God as our offering.

The fourth item of intrinsic significance concerns the Captain of Jehovah's army. The children of Israel were ready. They had been circumcised, they had enjoyed the Passover, and they had enjoyed the produce of the good land. However, they still needed a Captain. Then Joshua saw a vision in which Christ was unveiled as the Captain of Jehovah's army. Joshua was the visible commander, but Christ was the invisible One. Before the children of Israel attacked the Canaanites, they were fully prepared and qualified with Christ, the embodiment of God, as their Captain. When they attacked Jericho, they did this under the commanding of the Captain typified by the ark. The ark, a type of Christ, who was their Commander-in-chief, took the lead to attack the enemies.

To prepare to possess the good land, we need to enter into these four items. We need to deal with the flesh, enjoy the Lord's table, enjoy the all-inclusive Christ as the produce of the good land, and see a vision of Christ, the embodiment of God, as our Captain.

Now that we have seen the items of intrinsic significance in this chapter, let us consider some of the details concerning the preparation before the attack.

I. THE REACTION OF THE KINGS
OF THE AMORITES AND THE CANAANITES
TO JEHOVAH'S MIRACULOUS DEED
FOR ISRAEL TO CROSS OVER THE JORDAN

In verse 1 we see the reaction of the kings of the Amorites and the Canaanites to Jehovah's miraculous deed in drying up the waters for Israel to cross over the Jordan. Their hearts melted, and there was no longer any spirit (boldness) in them because of the children of Israel.

II. THE CIRCUMCISION OF THE NEW ISRAEL

Verses 2 through 9 speak of the circumcision of the new Israel.

A. At Gilgal

The circumcision of the new Israel took place at Gilgal, which means "a rolling." Concerning this, verse 9 says, "Then Jehovah said to Joshua, Today I have rolled away the reproach of Egypt from off you. So the name of this place has been called Gilgal to this day."

B. To Make God's Chosen People a New People
for the Inheritance of God's Promised Land

The purpose of circumcision was to make God's chosen people a new people for the inheritance of God's promised land (Gen. 17:7-12; Josh. 5:6).

C. Typifying the Circumcision of Christ,
by His Death, on the Believers

The circumcision of the new Israel typifies the circumcision of Christ, by His death, on the believers in the putting off of the body of the flesh for their inheritance, in resurrection, of Him as the God-allotted portion to them (Col. 2:9-12; 1:12).

III. THE KEEPING OF THE PASSOVER

Joshua 5:10 says that the children of Israel camped in Gilgal, and they kept the Passover on the fourteenth day of the month in the evening on the plains of Jericho.

A. To Remember Jehovah's Redemption of Israel from the Death Judgment on Their Firstborn Sons

The children of Israel were to keep the Passover to remember Jehovah's redemption of Israel from the death judgment on their firstborn sons (Exo. 12:3-7, 11-14).

B. To Remember Jehovah's Salvation of Israel from the Power of Pharaoh and Egypt

The keeping of the Passover was also to remember Jehovah's salvation of Israel from the power of Pharaoh and Egypt (Exo. 14:13-30).

C. Indicating That Jehovah Would Destroy the Tribes of Canaan and Deliver Israel from Them

The keeping of the Passover indicated that just as Jehovah had saved Israel from Pharaoh and Egypt so would He destroy the tribes of Canaan and deliver Israel from them. Thus the keeping of the Passover encouraged the children of Israel and gave them the assurance that Jehovah would displace the evil Canaanites.

D. Typifying the Believers' Keeping of the Lord's Table to Remember the Lord's Redemption and Salvation

Israel's keeping of the Passover typifies the believers' keeping of the Lord's table to remember the Lord's redemption and salvation (Matt. 26:26-28). The Lord Jesus established His table with the bread and the cup to replace the Feast of the Passover. He has fulfilled the type, and now He is the real Passover to us (1 Cor. 5:7).

IV. THE EATING OF THE PRODUCE
OF THE PROMISED LAND

Joshua 5:11-12 speaks of Israel's eating of the produce of the promised land.

A. Manna Having Been the Food from Heaven in Israel's Wandering in the Wilderness

Manna was the food from heaven in Israel's wandering in the wilderness. The manna typifies Christ as the unconsummated heavenly food to God's chosen people, not requiring the eaters to labor on it.

B. The Produce of the Promised Land Being the God-given Food in Their Fighting in Canaan

The produce of the promised land was the God-given food in their fighting in Canaan. This produce typifies Christ as the consummated God-given food to the believers, requiring them to labor on Him.

V. THE VISION SEEN BY JOSHUA

Joshua 5:13-15 is a record of the vision seen by Joshua.

A. Unveiling Christ to Joshua

Verse 13a says, "Now once, when Joshua was by Jericho, he lifted up his eyes and looked; and behold, there was a man standing opposite him, and His sword was drawn in His hand." This vision was an unveiling of Christ to Joshua.

B. Christ as the Captain of Jehovah's Army

Verses 13b and 14a go on to say, "Joshua went to Him and said to Him, Are You for us or for our adversaries? And He said, Neither, but as the Captain of Jehovah's army have I now come." Whereas Joshua was the visible captain of Jehovah's army, Christ was the invisible Captain of Jehovah's army. Christ was such a captain to fight against the seven tribes of Canaan for Israel. Because of this, Joshua needed to stand on the position of sanctification all the time (v. 15).

LIFE-STUDY OF JOSHUA

MESSAGE SIX

TAKING POSSESSION OF THE GOOD LAND FOR CHRIST AND BEING MADE HIS POSSESSION

Scripture Reading: Josh. 1:2-6; Phil. 3:8, 12; Rev. 2:7b; Josh. 5:12; Phil. 1:21; Eph. 1:11, 18

According to the divine revelation in the Scriptures, we need to take possession of the good land for Christ so that Christ can make us His possession. Our taking possession of the God-promised good land is for Christ, and Christ's making us His possession is for us. What does it mean to say that we possess the good land for Christ and that He, for our sake, makes us His possession? My burden in this message is to try to make these two puzzling matters clear.

OUR TAKING POSSESSION OF THE GOOD LAND FOR CHRIST

In the first message of this life-study, we pointed out that to take possession of the God-promised land for Christ and to provide the proper persons to bring forth Christ into the human race are the two major points of the section of the history in the Old Testament in the three books of Joshua, Judges, and Ruth. These two main points—to take the land for Christ and to provide the bona fide ancestors for Christ—are the spirit of the history from Joshua to Ruth. Since the God-promised land is a type of Christ, to gain the land for Christ means to gain Christ for Christ.

God's Promise concerning the Good Land

In Genesis God promised Abraham that He would give the good land to Abraham's descendants. More than four hundred years later, God sent Moses to deliver Israel out of Egypt, telling him that IIe was sending him to bring the people into the good land. It was a fact that God had given the land to Israel, but this fact was not yet practical. Rather, it was a promise that still needed to be fulfilled. Not even at the time when Israel came to the plains of Moab under the leadership of Joshua was the giving of the good land to Israel a practical fact, for the land had not yet become Israel's possession. Only after Israel had gained the good land and had taken possession of it did the land actually become theirs as a practical fact.

The Need for Us to Respond
to What God Has Promised, Prepared, and Given

The good land had been promised to Israel, and the situation was ready for the land to be given to Israel in actuality. God, the Giver, had done everything, but there was still the need for Israel, the receiver, to do something to take possession of what God had given.

The principle is the same with the preaching of the gospel today. God's salvation has been promised, prepared, and completed in Christ and with Christ. Everything is ready for this salvation to be given to sinners. God wants to give salvation to sinners, but they need to respond to Him by receiving His gift of salvation. To respond to God by receiving His salvation is to do something helpful for God. Actually, to receive God's salvation is to do God a favor. If you know the heart of God, you will realize that whenever a sinner repents and receives Christ, that sinner is doing God a favor.

At the beginning of the book of Joshua, Israel was ready to go forward, to take the good land, to possess it, and to enjoy it. For Israel to do this meant that they were doing something for Christ, who is typified by the good land. Otherwise, the good land would have lain there idle. Today, Christ as the good land is ready to be taken and possessed by His believers. However, where are those who are ready to take Him, possess Him, and enjoy Him as the all-inclusive good land? Many sinners are not willing to respond to Christ, and even many of His believers are not willing to respond to Him by taking Him, possessing Him, and enjoying Him.

Gaining Christ for Christ

In light of this, let us now consider what it means to gain Christ for Christ. Christ today is the good land given to us by God in a very rich way. Nevertheless, all the riches of Christ, all that Christ is, remain separate from most Christians. As the One on the throne in the heavens, Christ is strong and powerful, but we are weak. He is rich, but we are poor. Whereas Christ is strong, powerful, and rich, we are weak, impotent, and poor. The reason for this situation is that we have not endeavored to gain Christ. However, when we gain Christ, He becomes our experience. Then Christ becomes in us what He should be. This means that our gaining Christ is not only for our enjoyment but also for Christ to be what He should be.

According to the New Testament revelation, Christ is perfect, complete, rich, and powerful. Furthermore, it is a fact that God has given such a Christ to us. Although He is wonderful, we are pitiful. If we see this, we will realize that there is a need for us to do something that will make Christ real to us and even to the unbelievers so that He will be what He should be. How can Christ be what He should be? Christ can be what He should be only by our gaining Him. If we gain Christ and experience Christ, Christ will become real to us. This is not only for us—it is also for Christ. This is to gain Christ for Christ.

Our need today is to gain more of Christ, to possess more of Christ, and to experience more of Christ. Our gaining, possessing, and experiencing Christ will make Him real to us. This is not only for our enjoyment but also for Christ to be what He should be. At present, the Christ among us is much less than the Christ in the heavens. The Christ among us is different from the Christ in the heavens. This means that among us Christ is not yet what He should be. In order for Christ to be what He should be among us, we need to gain Him. The more we gain Christ, possess Christ, experience Christ, and enjoy Christ, the more He becomes among us what He should be. In this way our gaining of Christ is for Christ. We gain Christ for Christ so that He may have His corporate expression. This is to make the good land the land of Immanuel (Isa. 8:8).

God's Need for Overcomers Who Struggle to Pursue Christ in order to Gain Christ

Paul was one who struggled to pursue Christ in order to gain Christ (Phil. 3:8, 12). However, very few of today's Christians, including us, are like Paul. We may be seeking Christians, but we may pursue Christ only to a certain extent, being content with a routine church life and routine work and service for Christ. Following such a routine does not enable us to endeavor to gain Christ. Because so many Christians do not pursue Christ in order to gain Him, God needs the overcomers.

The Bible shows us that, first, God tried to work with the race of Adam, but the Adamic race was a failure. Then God had a new start with another race, with Israel, the race of Abraham. Eventually, Israel also failed God. Then God went to another people—the church. However, although God has been working with the church for nearly two thousand years, God has not yet gained what He desires. Thus, as early as the first century, the Lord came in to call for overcomers (Rev. 2:7, 11, 17, 26-28; 3:5, 12, 20-21; 21:7), and today He is still sounding out the call for the overcomers. Nevertheless, even among devoted Christians it is hard to find some overcomers, some who are pursuing Christ in order to gain Him.

At the time of Joshua, there were two or three million Israelites, but there were not many Joshuas and Calebs. There were not many endeavoring ones, genuine pursuers of God. Without such ones both the good land and the Giver of the land would have been idle. Both the land and the Giver of the land needed certain ones to take the land, possess the land, and enjoy the land. Those who possessed the land did a favor to the One who gave them the land.

We today need to take and possess the land for Christ. We need to gain Christ for Christ. If we do this, we will do Christ a favor. However, if we go on living a routine Christian life and church life, we will not be able to gain the land for Christ. For this, God needs some overcomers. There are millions of real Christians on earth today, but where are the overcomers? God is calling for overcomers, but who will answer His call? Who will respond to God's call by pursuing Christ in order to gain Christ? I hope that many among us will do Christ a favor by responding to God's call for overcomers.

CHRIST'S MAKING US HIS POSSESSION

When we enjoy Christ, He makes us His possession. This is something organic. If we take Christ, possess Christ, and enjoy Christ as our all-inclusive good land, the land will become our supply. What the land supplies us will cause us to become organic.

Becoming Organic by Being Constituted with Christ as the Food Produced through Our Labor on the Good Land

The main thing that the land affords us is food. If we do not have food, we cannot be organic. When we labor on the land, the land will produce food. Then we eat the food that is produced by our labor on the land, and as a result we become organic.

Anything that we take into us as food transforms us organically. When the Israelites were in Egypt, they ate Egyptian food, and this food caused them to have an Egyptian constitution. Eventually, God brought them out of Egypt and into the wilderness, where they remained for forty years. Every day while they were in the wilderness they ate something heavenly—manna. The manna constituted them into a heavenly people. Eventually, the manna ceased. Regarding this, Joshua 5:12 says, "The manna ceased on that day, when they ate of the produce of the land; and there was no longer manna for the children of Israel, but they ate of the yield of the land of Canaan that year." From that time onward, their constitution began to be different, for they began to be constituted with the produce of the good land. Thus, the children of Israel were constituted in three ways: first, in Egypt with Egyptian food; second, in the wilderness with manna; and third, in Canaan with the produce of the land. In each case they were constituted not by teachings or regulations but by what they ate.

As believers in Christ today, we also are constituted according to what we eat. If we want to be a heavenly people, we need to eat Christ as our heavenly manna. If we want to be overcomers, we need to labor on Christ as our good land. To labor on Christ means to gain Christ as our enjoyment. First, of course, we need to take the land. This requires that we dispossess the "Canaanites." After possessing Christ as the land, we need to labor on the land. Through our labor something will be produced, and that produce will become our food, our supply. As we eat Christ as this food and enjoy Him, we will be constituted with Him, being made the same as Christ in life and nature. This is what Paul meant when he said, "For to me, to live is Christ" (Phil. 1:21).

Transformed Metabolically
to Become God's Inheritance

This enjoyment of Christ will transform us metabolically and cause us to become Christ's treasure, His possession. Paul speaks of this in Ephesians 1. In this chapter we first have God's choosing and predestinating, and then we have Christ's redeeming. Through the redemption of Christ, we enter into Christ as a particular kind of element, and this element becomes our enjoyment that constitutes us into God's inheritance.

First, God comes into us to be our inheritance. When we enjoy Christ, He constitutes us to be God's inheritance. On the one hand, we have Christ as our good land, as our possession. On the other hand, the enjoyment of this possession constitutes us with Christ, and we thereby become God's inheritance.

An Organic Matter

The process of being constituted with Christ to become God's inheritance is altogether organic. This means that we need to take the all-inclusive Christ as our good land and labor on Him to gain some produce, which will be our organic, transforming food. As we eat this food, we will grow and gradually mature in the divine life. We will be constituted with Christ organically, transformed by Christ as a new element. Then in an organic way we will become God's inheritance, His treasure and possession.

LIFE-STUDY OF JOSHUA

MESSAGE SEVEN

THE DESTRUCTION OF JERICHO

Scripture Reading: Josh. 6

Joshua 6 is a record of the first warfare and destruction by Israel in the land of Canaan. In order for the children of Israel to gain the good land, they had to defeat the enemy and drive out the evil forces. Nevertheless, the children of Israel actually did not need to fight. When they crossed the Jordan, God did everything. In the same principle, God's people did not need to do anything to destroy Jericho. They only needed to believe and trust in God, to listen to the instruction from the Captain of the army of Israel, and to exalt Christ by bearing the ark. From this we see that in the spiritual warfare the first thing we should do is exalt Christ.

Jericho was strongly fortified. But when the king heard what Jehovah had done for His people, his heart melted and he lost his spirit, his boldness. Not knowing what to do, he shut the gates of the city and used the walls to protect himself and his people. There was no traffic, no coming in or going out. This indicates that the powers of darkness were bound, that there was a real binding of the spiritual forces of wickedness in the heavenly places. The king trusted in the wall, knowing that the Israelites did not have any weapons to breach the wall. Even though the Israelites had crossed the Jordan, he did not think that they would be able to cross the wall. He did not have any thought concerning what God would do. It was an easy matter for God to destroy the wall.

In verse 2 Jehovah told Joshua that He had given Jericho, its king, and the mighty men of war into Joshua's hand. Then God instructed Joshua to have the men of war with the priests bearing the ark circle the city, going around it one time. This they were to do for six days. Seven other priests

were charged to carry seven trumpets of rams' horns before
the ark of Jehovah. The priests did not blow their trumpets
according to their own will. Instead, they waited for the
captain to give the command. They needed instructions and
leading, just as we today need the leading and guiding of the
Spirit.

For the first six days, the army of Israel just walked
around the city with the ark, which typified Christ as the
embodiment of God. I believe that many of the people of
Jericho were on the wall watching, wondering what the
people of Israel were doing. On the seventh day, the Sabbath
day, the situation was different. Israel actually did not have to
fight but enjoyed the Sabbath, that is, enjoyed the rest. They
walked around the city seven times, and then the visible
captain gave the command: "Shout!" The priests trumpeted,
the people shouted, and the wall fell down. The city was
utterly destroyed, and a curse was placed on anyone who
would rise up and build it. The way that Israel conquered
Jericho was a strong testimony that Israel's God, Jehovah, is
a true and living God.

We may apply this account of the destruction of Jericho to
the matter of preaching the gospel. As we take up the burden
to visit sinners, we need to realize that every sinner is a
"fortified city" that has been cursed. In dealing with such
a fortified city, we must exercise patience, considering when
we should be silent and when we should speak. This means
that we should follow the Lord's leading. At the right time,
the proper declaration will be very effective, and there will be
a Sabbath day in which we can shout, "Praise the Lord! Jesus
is Lord! Christ is Victor!" The "wall" will fall, and we will be
able to defeat all the demons and possess that sinner for
Christ.

Let us now look at the various matters involved in the
destruction of Jericho as described in Joshua 6.

I. THE REACTION OF JERICHO TO ISRAEL

In verse 1 we see the reaction of Jericho to Israel. Jericho
was shut up tight because of the children of Israel. No one
went out and no one went in. The people of Jericho were

limited, unable to do anything. This indicates that even before Israel went up to take the city, Jericho was already defeated.

II. JEHOVAH'S PROMISE TO JOSHUA

According to verse 2 Jehovah promised Joshua that He had given Jericho and its king and its mighty men of war into his hand.

III. THE INSTRUCTION OF JEHOVAH, THE CAPTAIN OF HIS ARMY, TO JOSHUA

Verses 3 through 5 are a record of the instruction of Jehovah, the Captain of His army, to Joshua.

A. To Circle the City by All the Men of War

First, Jehovah charged Joshua to have all the men of war circle the city (v. 3a).

B. Going around the City Once a Day for Six Days

Jehovah instructed Joshua that the men of war were to go around the city once a day for six days (v. 3b).

C. Seven Priests Carrying Seven Trumpets of Rams' Horns before the Ark

Jehovah further instructed Joshua that seven priests were to carry seven trumpets of rams' horns before the ark (v. 4a).

D. On the Seventh Day Circling the City Seven Times, and the Priests Blowing the Trumpets

On the seventh day all the men of war were to circle the city seven times, and all the priests were to blow the trumpets (v. 4b). This signifies the declaring, the proclaiming, of Christ.

E. At the Hearing of the Trumpet Sound, All the People Shouting with a Great Shout

According to verse 5a, when the priests gave off the blast of the ram's horn and the people heard the trumpet sound, all the people were to shout with a great shout.

F. The Wall of the City Falling Down Flat, and the People Going Up

Jehovah went on to instruct Joshua that when the people shouted with a great shout, the wall of the city would fall down flat. Then they were to go up, each straight ahead (v. 5b).

IV. JOSHUA'S CHARGE TO THE PEOPLE ACCORDING TO JEHOVAH'S INSTRUCTION AND THE PEOPLE'S ACTION ACCORDING TO JEHOVAH'S CHARGE

Next, this chapter shows us Joshua's charge to the people according to Jehovah's instruction and the people's action according to Jehovah's charge (vv. 6-17a, 18-21, 24).

A. In Circling the City

In circling the city, the armed men passed on before the ark of Jehovah. The seven priests passed on before Jehovah and blew the trumpets, and the ark of Jehovah went after them. The armed men went before the priests who blew the trumpets, and the rearguard went after the ark, the trumpets continually blowing (vv. 6-9).

B. The People Not Shouting until the Day Joshua Told Them to Shout

Joshua commanded the people not to shout, nor to let their voice be heard, nor to let a word go forth from their mouth until the day he would say to them, "Shout!" Then they would shout (v. 10). There was a time to be silent, and there was a time to shout. Here, to be silent means to be one with the Lord to carry out the matter in the Lord's way without the expression of any thought, opinion, or feeling.

C. The Ark of Jehovah Circling the City Once a Day for Six Days and Seven Times on the Seventh Day

The ark of Jehovah circled the city, going around it one time, and did the same on the second day, circling the city one time. This they did for six days. Then on the seventh day they circled the city in the same manner seven times (vv. 11-15).

D. The People Shouting with a Great Shout, and the Wall Falling Down Flat

The seventh time they circled the city on the seventh day, the priests blew the trumpets, and Joshua said to the people, "Shout!" The people shouted with a great shout, and the wall fell down flat. Then the people went up into the city, each straight ahead, and they captured the city, utterly destroyed it with the edge of the sword, and burned it with fire (vv. 16, 20-21, 24a).

E. The Victory over Jericho Being Won by Israel's Blowing of the Trumpets and Shouting

The victory over Jericho in Israel's first battle after crossing the Jordan was won not by Israel's fighting but by their blowing of the trumpets and shouting, by their testifying and proclaiming of God with His ark, through their faith in God's word of instruction (vv. 2-5). These were the vital factors that enabled them to win the victory.

F. Not Taking Anything from the Destruction but Saving All the Silver, the Gold, and the Vessels of Bronze and Iron

They did not take anything from the destruction but saved all the silver, the gold, and the vessels of bronze and iron, sanctified them to Jehovah, and put them into the treasury of the house of Jehovah (vv. 18-19, 24b).

V. THE SALVATION RENDERED TO RAHAB AND HER HOUSEHOLD

This chapter speaks not only of the destruction of Jericho but also of the salvation rendered to Rahab and her household (vv. 17b, 22-23, 25). This was done in order to keep the promise that had been made to her (v. 22). Joshua preserved Rahab and her father's house and all that she had, and she remained within Israel (v. 25).

VI. THE OATH MADE BY THE PEOPLE
FOR THE CURSING OF JERICHO

Finally, this chapter tells us of the oath made by the people for the cursing of Jericho. "At that time Joshua charged the people with an oath, saying, Cursed be the man before Jehovah who raises up and builds this city Jericho! At the cost of his firstborn son shall he lay its foundation, and at the cost of his youngest son shall he set up its gates" (v. 26). This word was fulfilled with Hiel in 1 Kings 16:34.

LIFE-STUDY OF JOSHUA

THE DESTRUCTION OF AI

Scripture Reading: Josh. 7—8

In this message we will consider Joshua 7 and 8. These chapters give the account of the destruction of Ai.

The first time the children of Israel went up to destroy Ai they suffered a defeat. There were four reasons for this defeat. First, Israel sinned. God's people were to be holy, sanctified, especially during the time of war. But one of the men of war from the tribe of Judah sinned by stealing something that was devoted to destruction. Second, they lost the presence of the Lord. Third, they trusted in themselves. Fourth, they lost their oneness with God.

God can do everything without man, but according to the record of the book of Joshua He wants man to be one with Him. In keeping with the principle of incarnation, God wants to do everything through man, with man, and even in man. At Jericho Israel marched around the city with the ark, a type of Christ as the embodiment of the Triune God, on the shoulders of the priests. The spiritual significance of this scene is that it is a picture of a corporate God-man, God and man, man and God, walking together as one person. This was the way the children of Israel crossed the river Jordan, and this was the way they destroyed the city of Jericho. God and Israel were fighting together. Actually, however, God did the fighting, and Israel simply shouted, proclaimed, and testified and then occupied the city.

This scene should have continued through all the taking of the land. But after the destruction of Jericho, Israel sinned by taking something from Jericho that was devoted to destruction (6:18-19). Although this sin was committed by an individual, Achan, it affected the entire body of God's people.

For this reason God said to Joshua, "Israel has sinned" (7:11a). Because of this sin God stayed away from them, withdrawing His presence from them. This was the reason that Joshua and all the children of Israel became foolish, proud, and blind in attacking Ai.

At Jericho, according to God's economy, Joshua sent out spies, not for fighting but to gain Rahab. In the destruction of Jericho, no fighting was needed. But at Ai, because they lost the presence of the Lord, Joshua sent out spies for fighting (v. 2). The spies returned to Joshua and said that because the enemies were few, not all the people needed go up. They suggested that about two or three thousand men go up and strike Ai. Because of their foolishness, pride, and blindness, they despised their enemy. Nevertheless, Joshua received the report from the spies and sent three thousand men of war against Ai. But when Israel was defeated by the people of Ai and thirty-six men were slaughtered, Joshua realized that something was wrong. He then fell to the ground upon his face before the ark of Jehovah until evening (vv. 6-9).

God spoke to Joshua, telling him that unless they judged the sin, He would not be with them anymore (v. 12). Joshua called the people together, and through the Urim and Thummim he found the tribe (Judah), the family (Zerah), and the person (Achan) who had sinned (vv. 16-18). The children of Israel then stoned and burned Achan and all that he had. In this way Israel was cleared up and brought back to God to be one with God again.

We all need to learn a lesson from this account. We, the people of God, should always be one with our God. Today, especially in the New Testament, our God is not only among us but also within each one of us. Therefore, every one of us is not a solitary individual, a person alone. On the contrary, we are men with God, God-men. Do you realize that, as a believer in Christ, you are a God-man, that God is a part of your being and that you are a part of God's being? We come from many different countries, but we all are the same kind of person. We all are God-men. For this reason, we must realize that whatever we do, wherever we go, and whatever we are should not be by ourselves. We should not act, behave, or do things by ourselves but with God.

The report of the spies to Joshua indicates that Israel had set God aside. They forgot God and knew only themselves. At that time they were not one with God but cared only for themselves. Thus, God stayed away from them, and He said to Joshua, "I will not be with you anymore unless you destroy that which was devoted to destruction from among you" (v. 12c). It is a very serious matter for God no longer to be with us. Nothing can replace Him. I can testify that without God I cannot live. Apart from Him I cannot have any being.

Israel was separated from God because of their sin. This sin caused them to become foolish. Israel should have asked God what He wanted them to do against Ai. This was the secret for their victory. Joshua should have said to the people, "Do not forget what we experienced at Jericho. We did not fight, but instead we walked with God as one. Let us do the same thing at Ai, walking around the city with the ark." If Joshua had said this, he would have been a wise man, and the children of Israel would have followed his wise counsel.

The secret of Israel's defeat at Ai was that they lost God's presence and were no longer one with Him. After this defeat, Joshua learned the lesson of staying with the Lord before the ark. Eventually, the Lord came in to speak to him and to tell him what to do. The principle is the same with us today. If we have God's presence, we have wisdom, insight, foresight, and the inner knowledge concerning things.

As we study the intrinsic significance of this part of Israel's history, we need to learn the secret of walking with the Lord. Today we should not merely follow the Lord but walk with Him, living with Him and having our being with Him. This is the way to walk as a Christian, to fight as a child of God, and to build up the Body of Christ.

We need to remember that we are God-men and to practice being one with the Lord. Concerning this, the Lord Jesus said, "In that day you will know that I am in My Father, and you in Me, and I in you" (John 14:20). This word reveals that we are a people of "ins": we are in Christ and He is in us (15:4).

Therefore, whatever we do should not be done by ourselves but should be done with and by another One.

In my youth I was taught various ways to overcome, to be victorious, to be holy, and to be spiritual. However, not any of these ways worked. Eventually, through more than sixty-eight years of experience, I have found out that nothing works but the Lord's presence. His being with us is everything.

Let us now consider Joshua 7 and 8 in a more particular way.

I. THE DEFEAT AT AI

The defeat at Ai is described in chapter seven.

A. The Children of Israel Committing a Trespass in the Thing Devoted to Destruction

The children of Israel acted unfaithfully and committed a trespass in that which was devoted to destruction, for Achan took of that which was devoted to destruction. Concerning this, the anger of Jehovah was kindled against the children of Israel (v. 1).

B. Israel Acting on Their Own, without Seeking the Lord's Direction and without Having the Lord's Presence

Joshua sent men from Jericho to Ai, telling them to spy out the land. After they spied out Ai, they returned to Joshua and said to him, "Not all the people need go up; let about two or three thousand men go up and strike Ai. Do not make all the people labor there, for the enemies are few" (vv. 2-3). So only about three thousand men from the people went up there (v. 4a). This indicates that Israel acted on their own, without seeking the Lord's direction and without having the Lord's presence.

C. Israel Being Defeated and Driven Away by the Men of Ai

Israel was defeated and driven away by the men of Ai

(vv. 4b-5). As a result, "the heart of the people melted and became like water" (v. 5b).

D. The Anguish and Cry of Joshua and the Elders of Israel to Jehovah

In verses 6 through 9 we have the anguished cry of Joshua and the elders of Israel to Jehovah. Joshua rent his clothes and fell to the ground upon his face before the ark of Jehovah until the evening. The elders of Israel did likewise. Joshua said, "Ah, Lord Jehovah! Why have You brought this people over the Jordan at all, to give us over into the hand of the Amorites and cause us to perish? If only we had been content to dwell across the Jordan! Oh, Lord, what can I say after Israel has turned its back before its enemies?" (vv. 7-8). Joshua continued by asking Jehovah what He would do for His great name.

E. Jehovah's Charge

Verses 10 through 15 are a record of Jehovah's charge—to deal with the stealing of the thing devoted to destruction. Jehovah told Joshua that Israel had sinned, trespassing His covenant by taking that which had been devoted to destruction and putting it among their goods. That was the reason the children of Israel were not able to stand before their enemies but instead turned their backs before them. Jehovah went on to say that they would not be able to stand before their enemies until they removed from among them that which had been devoted to destruction. Jehovah charged that he who had stolen what was devoted to destruction was to be burned with fire, he and all that belonged to him.

F. Israel's Dealing with Their Sin

Verses 16 through 26 describe Israel's dealing with their sin.

1. Finding Out the One Who Committed the Sin

First, Israel found out the one who committed the sin (vv. 16-21). They did this by the Urim and the Thummim on the high priest's breastplate of judgment (Exo. 28:30). The

one who committed the sin was Achan, of the tribe of Judah.
When Joshua commanded him to say what he had done,
Achan replied, "It is true; I have sinned against Jehovah, the
God of Israel; and this is what I did: When I saw among the
spoil a beautiful mantle of Shinar and two hundred shekels of
silver and a wedge of gold weighing fifty shekels, I coveted
them and took them. And now they are hidden in the earth in
my tent, with the silver under it" (Josh. 7:20-21).

2. The Death Judgment
on the Sin by Stoning

Israel dealt with Achan by taking him, his sons and his
daughters, and all that he had and stoning them with stones
and burning them with fire. Then they erected over him a
great heap of stones, and Jehovah turned from the fierceness
of His anger (vv. 22-26).

II. THE VICTORY OVER AI

In 8:1-29 we see the victory over Ai.

A. Jehovah's Instruction

Verses 1 and 2 are Jehovah's instruction to Joshua regarding Ai. Jehovah charged Joshua not to be afraid or dismayed
but to take all the people of war with him to attack Ai.
Jehovah promised Joshua that He had given the king, the
people, the city, and the land of Ai into his hand. Then
Jehovah charged Joshua to do to Ai and its king as he had
done to Jericho and its king and to take the spoil and cattle of
Ai for Israel's plunder. Finally, Jehovah instructed Joshua
to set an ambush for the city of Ai behind it.

B. The Conquest and Destruction of Ai

In verses 3 through 29 we see the conquest and destruction of Ai. Joshua accomplished the attack according to
Jehovah's instruction (vv. 3-26, 28-29). Then Israel took the
cattle and the spoil of the city of Ai for themselves as plunder
according to what Jehovah had commanded Joshua (v. 27).

III. JOSHUA'S RECORDING AND READING OF THE LAW TO THE PEOPLE OF ISRAEL

Verses 30 through 35 are concerned with Joshua's recording and reading of the law to the people of Israel.

A. Building an Altar and Offering Burnt Offerings and Peace Offerings to Jehovah

Joshua built an altar to Jehovah, the God of Israel, on Mount Ebal, and they offered upon it burnt offerings to Jehovah and sacrificed peace offerings (vv. 30-31).

B. Writing the Law of Moses upon the Stones

There at Mount Ebal, in the presence of the children of Israel, Joshua wrote upon the stones a copy of the law of Moses (v. 32).

C. Blessing the People of Israel according to What Moses Had Commanded

Verse 33 speaks of the blessing of the people of Israel according to what Moses had commanded (Deut. 11:29-30; 27:11-13).

D. Reading the Entire Law to the Congregation of Israel

Finally, Joshua read the entire law of Moses, both the blessing and the curse, to the congregation of Israel (Josh. 8:34). Thus, verse 35 concludes, "There was not a word of all that Moses had commanded that Joshua did not read before all the congregation of Israel and the women and the little ones and the sojourners who went among them."

LIFE-STUDY OF JOSHUA

MESSAGE NINE

THE SAVING OF GIBEON

Scripture Reading: Josh. 9

To study the Old Testament histories and prophecies we need a full scope, a full view, of the entire Scriptures concerning God's economy for Christ and the church which consummates in the New Jerusalem. My burden in this message is to apply this principle to Joshua 9 so that we may see the intrinsic significance of this chapter.

Joshua 9 is a record of how the children of Israel were deceived by the Gibeonites. They were deceived because they were like a wife who forgot her husband. What they did here was exactly the same as what Eve did in Genesis 3. The subtle serpent wanted to tempt, to seduce, Adam, yet he did not dare to go to him directly. Instead, Satan went to Adam's counterpart, a female, because he knows that it is easier to deceive a female (2 Cor. 11:3; 1 Tim. 2:14).

The Bible reveals that in the universe there is a divine romance between God and His elect. The Bible is the record of a romance, in the most pure and holy sense, of a universal couple. The male of this couple is God Himself, and the female is God's redeemed people as a corporate being. The Bible shows us that we, as God's elect, are His wife and that between Him and us there must be a marriage union based upon mutual love. The universe, therefore, is a wedding place, the place where the Husband, the processed and consummated Triune God, is being joined in marriage to the redeemed, regenerated, sanctified, transformed, and glorified tripartite man. The Husband is triune and the wife is tripartite, and thus they match each other very well to live together as the unique couple in the entire universe. The consummation of this romance, of this married life, is seen in Revelation 21 and 22, two chapters that we need to read again and again until we have a clear view of the married life of this universal couple.

This divine romance is revealed repeatedly throughout the Bible. After man fell, God selected one man, Abraham. This one with all of his descendants, both Jewish and Gentile, became God's wife. In the Old Testament God often refers to Himself as the Husband and to His people as the wife (Isa. 54:5; 62:5; Jer. 2:2; 3:1, 14; 31:32; Ezek. 16:8; 23:5; Hosea 2:7, 19). Eventually, the Bible ends with the New Jerusalem as the ultimate consummation of God's elect in the new heaven and new earth, as the universal wife for eternity (Rev. 21:9-10).

In Jeremiah 2:2 Jehovah said to Israel, "I remember concerning you... / The love of your bridal days." There were some "bridal days," a period of time in which God "courted" Israel. By the time God had brought Israel out of Egypt to Sinai, surely she had "fallen in love" with this universal Man, this unique Hero. Whatever Israel wanted, He could do. What they needed, He had. He had the wisdom, the capacity, the ability, the strength, the might, the power, and the authority to do everything. He seemed to say to Israel, "I am the unique One for you, and I am sufficient for you. Since I am the best One, you should not go to anyone else but just take Me. I am the loving One, and you are My beloved." I believe that when Israel arrived at Sinai they made a definite determination to "marry" this One.

At Sinai they were married, and they went on together as a couple. Wherever they went, they were a couple walking together—the husband and the wife, the Triune God and His elect, walking as one. That was a picture of the God-man, partly God and partly man. The part that is God is the Husband, and the part that is man is the wife.

A wife should never leave her husband. Rather, she should always rely upon him and be one with him. If Eve had kept this principle when Satan came to seduce her, she would have run away to her husband. That would have been her protection, her safeguard.

Suppose I am a wife and a poor woman comes to me asking for some help. As a wife, should I do something directly, on my own, for this poor woman? Since this seems to be an insignificant matter, I might just give her a little money or some bread without asking my husband about it. This is what happened in Joshua 9. The Gibeonites came to Israel like a poor woman coming to a rich lady from a strong, high-ranking family. Israel, the wife, should have gone to her Husband and checked with Him. But Israel "did not ask for the counsel of Jehovah" (v. 14). Instead, Israel was deceived by the Gibeonites and made a covenant with them. Once the people of Israel had made this covenant, swearing to the Gibeonites by the name of Jehovah, the covenant could not be altered, and the Israelites could not touch the Gibeonites.

The real married life is when the wife is co-living with her husband, always one with him. This means that the only way to have a pleasant married life is for the wife to be one with her husband. However, this dear wife, Israel, never learned to be habitual in this matter. At Ai they suffered a defeat and learned the lesson to be one with the Lord, but they did not learn it fully. In chapter nine the Gibeonites came to them in a different way. Whereas the people of Ai fought against Israel strongly, the Gibeonites came to them begging to be their servants. The result was that Israel, this independent, individualistic wife, was deceived. She had no protection, no safeguard. From this chapter we need to learn that, as the Lord's wife, we should be one with Him all the time. This is the intrinsic significance of Joshua chapter nine.

Now that we have seen the intrinsic significance of this chapter, let us go on to consider what it says concerning the saving of Gibeon.

I. THE KINGS ACROSS THE JORDAN BEING THREATENED AND GATHERING TOGETHER TO FIGHT WITH ISRAEL

The kings who were across the Jordan in the hill country and in the lowland and on all the shore of the Great Sea toward Lebanon were threatened and gathered together to fight with Israel (vv. 1-2).

II. THE TRICK OF THE GIBEONITES

Verses 3 through 15 show us the trick of the Gibeonites.

A. Deceiving Israel with Craftiness

The Gibeonites deceived Israel with craftiness (vv. 3-13). They went out as though they were envoys, taking old sacks upon their donkeys, old torn up and bound up wineskins, old patched sandals on their feet, and old garments upon themselves. All the bread of their provisions was dry and had become moldy. They went to Joshua at the camp of Gilgal and said to him and to the men of Israel, "From a faraway land we have come; now therefore make a covenant with us" (v. 6). The men of Israel said to these Hivites, "Perhaps you dwell among us. How then can we make a covenant with you?" (v. 7). They told Joshua that they would be their servants. When Joshua asked them who they were and where they came from, they answered that they came from a very far land, having heard reports of Jehovah and of all that He had done in Egypt and to the two kings of the Amorites, Sihon king of Heshbon and Og king of Bashan. They went on to say that their elders and the inhabitants of their land told them to take provisions, go to meet the people of Israel, and say to them, "We will be your servants; make then a covenant with us" (v. 11). They claimed that their bread had been hot but was now moldy, that their wineskins were new but were now torn up, and that their clothes and sandals had become old because of the very long journey. From this we see that the Gibeonites acted craftily.

B. Israel Making Peace and a Covenant with Them to Let Them Live, without Asking the Counsel of Jehovah

The men of Israel took some of their provisions, but they did not ask for the counsel of Jehovah. Joshua then made peace with them and made a covenant with them to let them live. Furthermore, the leaders of the assembly swore an oath to them (vv. 14-15).

III. ISRAEL UNCOVERING THE TRICK

Eventually Israel uncovered the Gibeonites' trick (vv. 16-27). At the end of three days, after Israel had made a covenant with them, they heard that they were their neighbors and that they dwelt among them (v. 16).

A. Still Keeping Their Oath
because of the Faithfulness of Jehovah

Israel still kept their oath because of the faithfulness of Jehovah (vv. 16-20, 22-25). The children of Israel came to the cities of Gibeon, but they did not strike them, for the leaders of the assembly had sworn to them by Jehovah the God of Israel. When the assembly murmured against the leaders, they told the assembly that because they had sworn to the Gibeonites by Jehovah, they could not touch them. They let them live so that wrath would not come upon Israel because of the oath that they had sworn to the Gibeonites.

Joshua called for the Gibeonites and asked them why they had deceived Israel by saying that they were far from them when they actually dwelt among them. The Gibeonites told Joshua that they knew that Jehovah the God of Israel had commanded Moses His servant to give all the land to Israel and to destroy all the inhabitants of the land. Then they said, "Therefore we were very afraid for our lives because of you, and we did this thing. And now here we are in your hand: Do as it seems good and upright in your sight to do to us" (vv. 24b-25).

B. Taking Them as Slaves

Joshua delivered the Gibeonites from the hand of the children of Israel, and they did not slay them. Instead, Joshua took the Gibeonites as slaves—woodcutters and drawers of water for all the assembly and for the house of God and for the altar of Jehovah (vv. 21, 23, 26-27).

IV. INDICATING THAT JEHOVAH HAD MADE
HIS ELECT, ISRAEL, POWERFUL
BEFORE THE EYES OF ALL THE CANAANITES

This account of the saving of Gibeon indicates that Jehovah had made His elect, Israel, powerful before the eyes of all the Canaanites.

LIFE-STUDY OF JOSHUA

MESSAGE TEN

THE DESTRUCTION
OF ALL THE REST OF THE NATIONS
IN THE HILL COUNTRY
AND THE LOWLAND WEST OF THE JORDAN
AND ON ALL THE SHORE OF THE GREAT SEA

Scripture Reading: Josh. 10—12

We all need to learn how to study the Bible. In studying the Bible, we should not understand it merely according to letters nor according to the natural way by the natural mind. The Bible has its spirit, reality, and center. Therefore, we need to learn how to know the center, reality, lines, and principles of the Word of God. We should keep this in mind as we come to Joshua 10 through 12. My burden in this message is that we would see the intrinsic significance of these chapters.

Joshua 10 through 12 show Joshua's destruction of all the rest of the nations in the hill country and the lowland west of the Jordan and on all the shore of the great sea. The strongest people in Canaan were in a strip of land from Lebanon in the north to Egypt in the south and from the Mediterranean Sea to the river Jordan. These people included the Anakim, a race of giants. According to Numbers 13:33, the sons of Anak were from the Nephilim. Genesis 6 reveals that the Nephilim were the issue of the evil union between the daughters of men and fallen angels. Because of the Nephilim, God charged His elect to slaughter everyone in the land. God is kind, loving, and merciful, but He is also severe because He has an enemy on earth.

God made the earth in His economy, and He purposely created a strip of land between the River Jordan and the Mediterranean Sea. God promised this land to Abraham and his descendants. Eventually, this land became the land of Christ, the land of Immanuel (Isa. 8:8). But when Israel was ready to take possession of Canaan, it was filled with demon-possessed people, idol worshippers, and Nephilim. Joshua slaughtered them (Josh. 11:21-22), but some on the mountain were quite strong, so Caleb came in and conquered them (14:6-14).

The significance of this is that without Joshua we cannot fully understand the spiritual warfare in Ephesians 6. There is spiritual warfare in the invisible scene behind the visible scene. This means that in addition to war on the earth, there is a war between God and Satan in the air. The heavenlies are full of Satan's forces. Christ is our good land, and God wants us to gain Christ, but there is a layer of devilish, demonic forces between us and the good land. If we would take possession of the good land for our enjoyment, we have to defeat these satanic forces.

Joshua conquered many nations and killed many kings, but he conquered only a narrow strip of land. According to Joshua 1, the land stretched from the Mediterranean to the Euphrates. The good land was wide and spacious; however, Israel's territory never spread to the Euphrates. Since there was much fighting and rebellion after the time of Joshua, there was not the opportunity for God's people to build a temple. When David gained more land and there was a time of peace, Solomon, David's son, was able to build the temple of God to set up God's kingdom on earth.

In principle, our situation is the same in the Lord's recovery today. Our standing on the church ground annuls the standing of all the denominations, and this stirs up opposition. We are God's Israel, and we have our Captain, but the Lord's recovery is still involved in a struggle. Every day we need to engage in spiritual warfare.

In the United States there are more than two hundred and fifty churches, but nearly all of them are small. It is hard to get an increase. There is a struggle in the United States because it is a crucial country, affecting the entire world situation related to the Lord's move. Our enemies are not humans on the earth but evil forces in the air, who hinder people from believing into the name of the Lord Jesus and who frustrate the saved ones from pursuing Christ to the uttermost.

We all need to know what the recovery is, where the recovery is, and what kind of persons can take the recovery on. We all need to see that in the Lord's recovery today we are on a battlefield. We should be today's Joshua and Caleb, fighting against Satan's aerial forces so that we can gain more of Christ for the building up of the Body of Christ, setting up and spreading the kingdom of God so that Christ can come back to inherit the earth. It is not adequate for us simply to be spiritual and holy. We need to learn of Joshua and Caleb to represent God's interest in this age to fight down the enemies that Christ can be gained by people and that Christ can be increased by His pursuers.

Let us now consider a number of the details in Joshua 10 through 12.

I. THE DESTRUCTION OF JERUSALEM, HEBRON, JARMUTH, LACHISH, AND EGLON

Joshua 10:1-27 records the destruction of Jerusalem, Hebron, Jarmuth, Lachish, and Eglon.

A. The King of Jerusalem Being Threatened by Israel's Destruction of Jericho and Ai and Their Peaceful Agreement with Gibeon

The king of Jerusalem was threatened by Israel's destruction of Jericho and Ai and their peaceful agreement with Gibeon (vv. 1-2). When he heard that Joshua had taken Ai and had utterly destroyed it as he had done to Jericho and that the inhabitants of Gibeon had made peace with Israel and were among them, he was afraid, knowing that Gibeon was a great city and that all its men were mighty men.

B. The Kings of the Five Nations Forming an Alliance to Fight against Gibeon

The kings of the five nations formed an alliance to fight against Gibeon. The king of Jerusalem sent word to the kings of Hebron, Jarmuth, Lachish, and Eglon, saying to them, "Come up to me and help me, and let us strike Gibeon; for they have made peace with Joshua and the children of Israel" (v. 4). Thus the five kings of the Amorites went up to Gibeon and fought against it.

C. Israel Engaging in War against the Five Nations

In verses 6 through 27 we see that Israel engaged in war against the five nations.

1. The Gibeonites Begging Israel to Fight for Them against the Five Nations

The Gibeonites begged Israel to fight for them against the five nations (v. 6).

2. Jehovah Encouraging Joshua to Defeat Them

Jehovah encouraged Joshua to defeat these nations, saying to him, "Do not be afraid of them, for I have given them into your hand. No man among them will stand before you" (v. 8). Joshua came upon them suddenly, and Jehovah threw them into a panic before Israel, struck them with a great stroke, and pursued them.

3. Jehovah Sending Hailstones to Destroy Them

While the five nations fled from before Israel, "Jehovah sent large stones upon them from heaven as far as Azekah, and they died. There were more who died because of the hailstones than the children of Israel slew with the sword" (v. 11).

4. Jehovah Causing the Sun and the Moon to Stay Still for about a Whole Day

Jehovah caused the sun and the moon to stay still for about a whole day (vv. 12-14). These two miracles by Jehovah were by natural forces.

5. *Joshua and the Children of Israel Destroying the People of the Five Nations and Killing Their Kings*

Joshua and the children of Israel destroyed the people of the five nations and killed their kings (vv. 15-27). The five kings were brought out of the cave into which they had fled, and Joshua told the chiefs of the men of war who were with him to put their feet on the necks of these kings. They did so, and Joshua said to them, "Do not be afraid or dismayed; be strong and be bold, for thus will Jehovah do to all your enemies against whom you fight" (v. 25).

II. THE DESTRUCTION OF THE THIRTY-ONE KINGS OF THE THIRTY-ONE NATIONS IN THE HILL COUNTRY AND THE LOWLAND WEST OF JORDAN

Joshua 10:28—12:24 is a record of the destruction of the thirty-one kings of the thirty-one nations in the hill country and the lowland west of the Jordan, from Baal-gad in the valley of Lebanon unto Mount Halak going up to Seir.

A. Jehovah, the God of Israel, Fighting for Israel

Joshua 10:42 says that Joshua took all these kings and their lands at one time, "for Jehovah, the God of Israel, fought for Israel." When certain other kings came together to fight with Israel, Jehovah said to Joshua, "Do not be afraid because of them, for tomorrow at this time I will deliver all of them up slain before Israel" (11:6a).

B. According to the Command of Moses the Servant of Jehovah

Joshua took all the cities of these kings with their kings, struck them with the edge of the sword, and utterly destroyed them. This he did according to the command of Moses the servant of Jehovah (v. 12). Verse 15 says, "As Jehovah had commanded Moses His servant, so Moses commanded Joshua, and so Joshua did; he left nothing undone of all that Jehovah had commanded Moses." Therefore, Joshua took the whole land according to all that Jehovah had spoken to Moses (v. 23).

C. According to God's Intention

The destruction of the thirty-one kings of the thirty-one nations was according to God's intention. Concerning this, verse 20 says, "It was of Jehovah to harden their heart to meet Israel in battle so that He might utterly destroy them and that they might not receive mercy but be destroyed as Jehovah commanded Moses." From this we see that God's intention was not to have mercy on these kings but to destroy them.

1. Israel Burning None of the Cities That Stood on Their Mounds except Hazor

Verse 13 says that Israel burned none of the cities that stood on their mounds except Hazor.

2. Some of the Anakim Being Left in Gaza, Gath, and Ashdod

Some of the Anakim were left in Gaza, Gath, and Ashdod (v. 22; cf. Num. 13:33).

III. THE DESTRUCTION OF HESHBON UNDER KING SIHON AND BASHAN UNDER KING OG EAST OF THE JORDAN

Joshua 12:1-6 speaks of the destruction of Heshbon under King Sihon and Bashan under King Og east of the Jordan.

A. By Moses and the Children of Israel

The destruction of Heshbon and Bashan was by Moses and the children of Israel (v. 6a).

B. Before Israel's Crossing of Jordan

This destruction took place before Israel's crossing of Jordan (v. 1a).

C. Given by Moses to the Tribes of Reuben and Gad and the Half-tribe of Manasseh

The land of Heshbon under King Sihon and of Bashan under King Og was given by Moses to the tribes of Reuben and Gad and the half-tribe of Manasseh (v. 6b).

LIFE-STUDY OF JOSHUA

MESSAGE ELEVEN

THE ALLOTMENT OF THE LAND

(1)

Scripture Reading: Josh. 13—17

Within God's economy there is such a thing as the allotment of the land. After Joshua took possession of the land, God commanded him to allot the land that had been possessed and even the land that had not yet been possessed, because in God's eyes all the land was for Israel. In this message we will begin to consider the allotment of the land. In particular, we will endeavor to see the intrinsic significance of the allotment of the good land.

In His wisdom, God did not allot the good land as a whole to all the children of Israel. Rather, He allotted the land, that is, Christ, to the different tribes. All the tribes were not the same; they were different.

In Genesis 49 Jacob, the father of the twelve tribes, blessed each of his sons in the form of a prophecy (see *Life-study of Genesis*, Messages 98-107). Jacob's blessing of Judah reveals that God considered Judah a threefold lion: a lion's whelp, a mature lion, and a lioness (v. 9). As a whelp he could grow and become strong, as a lion he could fight, and as a lioness he could produce. Benjamin was a ravenous wolf (v. 27), and Dan was a serpent on the way, biting the horses' heels to frustrate God's people from going on (v. 17). Zebulun was a haven of ships (v. 13), and Naphtali was a hind let loose (v. 21).

Because the tribes were different, God could not give the same land in the same way to every tribe. All the tribes were possessors of the land, but the tribes possessed particular portions of the land according to what they were. The top portion of the land was allotted to Judah. Dan was allotted a portion, but they did not dispossess the occupying Canaanites. They were God's people, yet in their actions they were in the principle of God's enemy.

The fulfillment of this type of the allotment of the land is among us today. We all have the same Christ, but we experience Christ in different ways. The land (Christ) we possess is according to what we are.

In Leviticus 1 Christ is unveiled as burnt offerings in five types: a bullock, a sheep from the flock, a goat, a turtledove, and a young pigeon. These items typify just one Christ, but they were offered according to the offerer's ability, indicating that our experiences of Christ differ in both size and kind. The size and kind do not depend on Christ but on our experience and enjoyment of Christ. Whereas the Christ experienced by Paul was typified by a bullock, the Christ experienced by many believers today is typified by a pigeon.

Christ is also unveiled by the three kinds of meal offerings in Leviticus 2: fine flour, a wafer, and grain that remains in the ears. If we are weak and cannot eat the wafer, we can eat the fine flour. As we grow we can experience Christ as the wafer. The apostle Paul was fully mature and full of energy. He was one who ate the grain. Once again we see that there is only one Christ—one Christ in many types and sizes—but we may experience Him in different ways and in different degrees as fine flour, a wafer, and grain.

The intrinsic significance of the allotment of the land is that the possessors of the land are different. This indicates that the experience of Christ among God's people is not the same. In God's ordination the good land is allotted to His people in different degrees. The New Testament clearly tells us that "God has apportioned to each a measure of faith" (Rom. 12:3). We are also told that "all the members do not have the same function" (v. 4). Therefore, God gives grace to each member according to its function in the Body (Eph. 4:7). This is God's ordination and the divine allotment.

Our hymnal, which was compiled in 1963 and 1964, illustrates this allotment. I would ask you to compare John Nelson

Darby's hymn on the exaltation of Christ (*Hymns,* #127) with Charles Wesley's hymn on the incarnation of Christ (#84). Here is the text of Darby's hymn:

1 Hark! ten thousand voices crying,
   "Lamb of God!" with one accord;
   Thousand thousand saints replying,
   Wake at once the echo'ng chord.

2 "Praise the Lamb!" the chorus waking,
   All in heav'n together throng;
   Loud and far each tongue partaking
   Rolls around the endless song.

3 Grateful incense this, ascending
   Ever to the Father's throne;
   Every knee to Jesus bending,
   All the mind in heav'n is one.

4 All the Father's counsels claiming
   Equal honors to the Son,
   All the Son's effulgence beaming,
   Makes the Father's glory known.

5 By the Spirit all pervading,
   Hosts unnumbered round the Lamb,
   Crowned with light and joy unfading,
   Hail Him as the great "I AM."

6 Joyful now the new creation
   Rests in undisturbed repose,
   Blest in Jesus' full salvation,
   Sorrow now nor thraldom knows.

7 Hark! the heavenly notes again!
   Loudly swells the song of praise;
   Through creation's vault, Amen!
   Amen! responsive joy doth raise.

Let us now consider the text of Wesley's hymn:

1 Hark! the herald angels sing,
     "Glory to the new-born King;
   Peace on earth and mercy mild;
     God and sinners reconciled."
   Joyful, all ye nations, rise,
     Join the triumph of the skies;
   With angelic hosts proclaim,
     "Christ is born in Bethlehem."

2 Christ, by highest heav'n adored,
     Christ, the everlasting Lord:
   Late in time behold Him come,
     Offspring of a virgin's womb.
   Veiled in flesh the Godhead see,
     Hail th' incarnate Deity!
   Pleased as man with man to dwell,
     Jesus our Immanuel.

3 Hail the heav'n-born Prince of Peace!
     Hail the Sun of righteousness!
   Light and life to all He brings,
     Ris'n with healing in His wings:
   Mild He lays His glory by,
     Born that man no more may die;
   Born to raise the sons of earth;
     Born to give them second birth.

4 Come, Desire of nations, come!
     Fix in us Thy humble home:
   Rise, the woman's conqu'ring seed,
     Bruise in us the serpent's head;
   Adam's likeness now efface,
     Stamp Thine image in its place:
   Final Adam from above,
     Reinstate us in Thy love.

As we compare these two hymns, we see that Darby's hymn is higher than Wesley's. This indicates that Darby's experience of Christ as expressed in his hymn was higher than Wesley's as expressed in his hymn. Although both Darby and Wesley experienced Christ as a bullock, Darby's bullock was larger than Wesley's.

If we go on to compare their experiences of Christ with the experience expressed in *Hymns*, #551, we will see that this hymn expresses a much lower experience of Christ:

1 I've believed the true report,
    Hallelujah to the Lamb!
 I have passed the outer court,
    O glory be to God!
 I am all on Jesus' side,
 On the altar sanctified,
 To the world and sin I've died,
    Hallelujah to the Lamb!

    Hallelujah! Hallelujah!
    I have passed the riven veil,
    Here the glories never fail,
    Hallelujah! Hallelujah!
    I am living in the presence
      of the King.

2 I'm a king and priest to God,
    Hallelujah to the Lamb!
 By the cleansing of the blood,
    O glory be to God!
 By the Spirit's pow'r and light,
 I am living day and night,
 In the holiest place so bright,
    Hallelujah to the Lamb!

3 I have passed the outer veil,
    Hallelujah to the Lamb!
 Which did once God's light conceal,
    O glory be to God!
 But the blood has brought me in
 To God's holiness so clean,
 Where there's death to self and sin,
    Hallelujah to the Lamb!

4 I'm within the holiest pale,
    Hallelujah to the Lamb!
  I have passed the inner veil,
    O glory be to God!
  I am sanctified to God
  By the power of the blood,
  Now the Lord is my abode,
    Hallelujah to the Lamb!

The hymns in our hymnal are arranged according to theological order and according to spiritual experience. Of the original 1080 hymns in our hymnal, approximately 700 were selected from many different hymnals. Among these hymns there was something lacking concerning the all-inclusive and all-extensive Christ, the compound life-giving Spirit of Christ, the divine life, and the church. To fill this lack, we composed more than 200 new hymns on Christ, the Spirit, life, and the church. Consider, for example, *Hymns,* #499:

1 Oh, what a life! Oh, what a peace!
  The Christ who's all within me lives.
  With Him I have been crucified;
  This glorious fact to me He gives.
  Now it's no longer I that live,
  But Christ the Lord within me lives.

2 Oh, what a joy! Oh, what a rest!
  Christ now is being formed in me.
  His very nature and life divine
  In my whole being inwrought shall be.
  All that I am came to an end,
  And all of Christ is all to me.

3 Oh, what a thought! Oh, what a boast!
  Christ shall in me be magnified.
  In nothing shall I be ashamed,
  For He in all shall be applied.
  In woe or blessing, death or life,
  Through me shall Christ be testified.

4 Oh, what a prize! Oh, what a gain!
  Christ is the goal toward which I press.
  Nothing I treasure, nor aught desire,
  But Christ of all-inclusiveness.
  My hope, my glory, and my crown
  Is Christ, the One of peerlessness.

The words of this hymn are simple, but they are very rich
concerning the experience of Christ as life. This shows that
the hymns in the Lord's recovery are full of truth and touch
the experience of Christ in a rich way, indicating our rich
divine allotment.

Hymns are poetry, and every poem is an expression of the
writer's sentiment. The word *sentiment* means more than just
a feeling. This word implies feeling, realization, understanding, and appreciation. The more we consider our sentiment,
the more we will have the burden to write poetry. The kind of
sentiment expressed in a particular hymn is a measure of
that writer's enjoyment of Christ; it indicates the "size" of the
Christ experienced and enjoyed by that writer. Thus, Wesley
wrote his hymn on the incarnation of Christ according to his
sentiment, and Darby wrote his hymn on the exaltation of
Christ according to his sentiment. Both hymns were written
according to the measure of the Christ enjoyed by the writers.

At this point I would like to say a word concerning
Hymns, #132, a hymn on the exaltation of Christ written by
me according to my sentiment:

1 Lo! in heaven Jesus sitting,
    Christ the Lord is there enthroned;
  As the man by God exalted,
    With God's glory He is crowned.
2 He hath put on human nature,
    Died according to God's plan,
  Resurrected with a body,
    And ascended as a man.
3 God in Him on earth was humbled,
    God with man was domiciled;
  Man in Him in heav'n exalted,
    Man with God is reconciled.

4 He as God with man is mingled,
  God in man is testified;
  He as man with God is blended,
  Man in God is glorified.

5 From the Glorified in heaven
  The inclusive Spirit came;
  All of Jesus' work and Person
  Doth this Spirit here proclaim.

6 With the Glorified in heaven
  Is the Church identified;
  By the Spirit of this Jesus
  Are His members edified.

7 Lo! a man is now in heaven
  As the Lord of all enthroned;
  This is Jesus Christ our Savior,
  With God's glory ever crowned!

If we consider what this hymn says regarding Christ's being God mingled with man, His putting on human nature, His dying according to God's plan, His resurrecting with a body, His ascending as a man, His sitting in the heavens, and His being crowned with God's glory, we will realize that this hymn is full of truth and enlightenment. This hymn is an expression of my holy, heavenly, and spiritual sentiment; it is an expression of the Christ whom I know and whom I have gained, experienced, and enjoyed.

We have seen that the intrinsic significance of the allotment of the good land is that we, the possessors of the land, experience the one Christ in different ways. Let us now consider the details concerning the allotment of the land described in chapters thirteen through seventeen.

I. THE LAND REMAINING TO BE POSSESSED

Joshua 13:1-7 speaks of the land that remained to be possessed. When Joshua was old, Jehovah said to him, "You are old and advanced in age, and very much of the land remains to be possessed" (v. 1).

A. The Regions of the Land
That Remained to Be Possessed

The regions of the land that remained to be possessed included that of the Philistines, the Geshurites, the Canaanites, and the Gebalites and all of Lebanon (vv. 2-6a).

B. Jehovah's Promise

In verse 6b we have Jehovah's promise that He would drive out all the inhabitants of the remaining land before the children of Israel.

C. Joshua Being Charged to Allot
the Remaining Land West of the Jordan

Jehovah charged Joshua to allot the remaining land to Israel as an inheritance as He had commanded him. Jehovah told Joshua to divide this land as an inheritance to the nine tribes and the half-tribe of Manasseh (vv. 6c-7; 14:1-2).

II. THE LAND EAST OF THE JORDAN
ALLOTTED TO THE TWO AND A HALF TRIBES BY MOSES

The land east of the Jordan had been allotted to the two and a half tribes by Moses (13:8-13, 15-32; 14:3a).

III. NO LAND ALLOTTED TO THE TRIBE OF LEVI

No land was allotted to the tribe of Levi because the offerings of Jehovah, the God of Israel, were their inheritance (13:14). Verse 33 goes on to say that the God of Israel would be the inheritance of the tribe of Levi. Thus, the children of Israel divided the land as Jehovah had commanded Moses. They gave no portion to the Levites in the land, but only cities to dwell in with their pasture lands for cattle and their substance (14:4-5).

IV. THE LAND ALLOTTED TO THE TRIBE OF JUDAH

Joshua 14:6—15:63 describes the land allotted to the tribe of Judah.

A. The Claim of Caleb

The first matter covered here was the claim of Caleb (14:6-15; 15:13-19). Caleb claimed Hebron with the hill country (14:10-15). His claim was according to the oath of Moses and the promise of Jehovah (14:6-9a; Num. 14:24; 32:12; Deut. 1:36). This land was promised to Caleb because he had fully followed Jehovah his God (Josh. 14:9b). Caleb took possession of the land promised to him by Moses and Jehovah (15:13-15), and then Caleb's son-in-law gained the springs in the region of the land (vv. 16-19).

B. The Extreme Southern Part of the Good Land

The lot for the tribe of the children of Judah extended to the border of Edom, to the wilderness of Zin at the south, the extreme southern part of the good land (15:1).

C. One Hundred Twelve Cities with Their Towns and Villages

The land allotted to the tribe of Judah included one hundred twelve cities with their towns and villages (vv. 21-62).

D. The Children of Judah Being Unable to Dispossess the Jebusites

The children of Judah were unable to dispossess the Jebusites, the inhabitants of Jerusalem, who dwelt with the children of Judah in Jerusalem (v. 63).

V. THE LAND ALLOTTED TO THE TRIBE OF JOSEPH

Chapters sixteen and seventeen describe the land allotted to the tribe of Joseph.

A. From Jericho to Bethel and to the Sea

The lot for the children of Joseph went from Jericho to Bethel and to the sea (16:1-4).

B. The Land Allotted to the Children of Ephraim, the Second Son of Joseph

1. From Jericho through the River Jordan to the Sea

The land allotted to the children of Ephraim, the second son of Joseph, went from Jericho through the river Jordan to the sea (vv. 5-8).

2. With the Cities in the Midst of the Inheritance of the Children of Manasseh

This allotted land was together with the cities with their villages set apart for the children of Ephraim in the midst of the inheritance of the children of Manasseh (v. 9).

3. Not Dispossessing the Canaanites Who Dwelt in Gezer

The children of Ephraim did not dispossess the Canaanites who dwelt in Gezer. Thus, the Canaanites dwelt in the midst of Ephraim and became forced labor (v. 10).

C. The Land Allotted to Manasseh, the Firstborn of Joseph

In 17:1-18 we have an account of the land allotted to Manasseh, the firstborn of Joseph.

1. Gilead and Bashan Having Been Allotted to Machir, the Firstborn of Manasseh

Gilead and Bashan, east of the Jordan, were allotted to Machir, the firstborn of Manasseh (vv. 1b, 5b, 6b).

2. The Land Allotted to the Rest of the Children of Manasseh

The land allotted to the rest of the children of Manasseh went south to Ephraim, west to the sea, north to Asher, and east to Issachar (vv. 1a, 2, 5a, 7-10).

3. Manasseh Having Some Cities with Their Towns in the Land of the Tribes of Issachar and Asher

Manasseh also had some cities with their towns in the land of the two tribes of Issachar and Asher (v. 11).

4. The Daughters of Zelophehad Claiming an Inheritance among Their Brothers

Zelophehad, the fourth generation of Manasseh, had no sons but daughters. His daughters claimed an inheritance among their brothers according to Jehovah's command to Moses (vv. 3-5a, 6a; Num. 27:1-11).

5. The Children of Manasseh Being Unable to Dispossess the Cities in Their Land

The children of Manasseh were unable to dispossess the cities in their land, but the Canaanites persisted in dwelling in the land. When the children of Manasseh became strong, they made the Canaanites forced labor, but they did not utterly dispossess them (Josh. 17:12-13).

6. The Children of Joseph Requesting More Land

The children of Joseph requested more land because they were a numerous people. Joshua encouraged them to dispossess the hill country with its valley, though the Canaanites had chariots of iron and were strong (vv. 14-18).

LIFE-STUDY OF JOSHUA

MESSAGE TWELVE

THE ALLOTMENT OF THE LAND

(2)

Scripture Reading: Josh. 18—22

Many spiritual items concerning Christ and the church are revealed in the New Testament in principle but not in detail. This is especially true in the matter of gaining Christ, experiencing Christ, and enjoying Christ.

In the book of Ephesians Christ is revealed as being all-inclusive because He is the One who fills all in all (Eph. 1:23). He is not only all-inclusive but also all-extensive because His love is immeasurable in its breadth, length, height, and depth (3:18-19a). Christ's love is just Himself. If His love is immeasurable, He is immeasurable. In Ephesians 3:8 Paul speaks of the unsearchable riches of Christ. His riches are so plentiful and vast that they are untraceable. Although Ephesians reveals a Christ who is all-inclusive, all-extensive, and unsearchably rich, in this book we cannot find the detailed ways to gain this Christ.

The detailed ways to gain Christ, experience Christ, and enjoy Christ are not in the New Testament. However, Joshua 13—22 provides the detailed way to possess and enjoy the land, which is a type of the all-inclusive Christ.

The good land was spacious, stretching from the Mediterranean Sea to the Euphrates, but the children of Israel did not possess all the land. Even with what they possessed, they still needed a detailed way to allot the land in order to gain and enjoy it. The way was by casting lots. In the book of Joshua the word *lot* is used in the sense of casting lots (18:8, 10). Humanly speaking, we know that casting lots depends on fortune, but God is our fortune, and the outcome of the casting of lots was according to what He had ordained. When God created the earth, He had a clear view concerning the situation of the good land. He was clear, for instance, that Jerusalem and the surrounding district were for Judah, out of whom Christ would come. This was foreordained, but it still had to be realized by casting lots. God's ordaining hand was present in the casting of lots to direct the result. This means that the division of the land did not depend upon Joshua, upon the high priest, or upon anyone other than God. As a result, there was no ground for the tribes to complain about the portion of the land allotted to them. The way of allotting the land was fair, and it caused everyone to be subdued.

At this juncture, I would like to emphasize the fact that Christ in Himself is uniquely one and always the same. As to Himself there is no change; He is the same yesterday, today, and forever (Heb. 13:8). However, in our experience and enjoyment Christ is of many sizes and types, as indicated by the different kinds of burnt offerings and meal offerings. What Christ is to us in our experience does not depend upon Him—it depends upon us. We gain Christ, experience Christ, and enjoy Christ according to what we are. Therefore, someone who is diligent in pursuing Christ will experience a larger Christ than someone who is lazy in this matter.

Recently I have been considering that we may regard the twelve tribes of Israel as a picture of the believers from the first century until today. Galatians 6:16 says that we are "the Israel of God." This indicates that among God's New Testament elect there should be twelve "tribes." The first tribe was the early apostles, who brought in the New Testament revelation. The second tribe was the church fathers. The third tribe was the martyrs in the Roman Empire. The fourth tribe was the reformers in the Roman Church, before the papal system was established. The fifth tribe was the Protestants, and the sixth was the mystics. The Protestants became shallow and dead, so there was a reaction from the mystics, including Madame Guyon, Father Fenelon, and Brother Lawrence. The seventh tribe was the Moravian brothers under Count Zinzendorf. The eighth tribe was the British Brethren under

John Nelson Darby. When the Brethren became full of dead knowledge, there was a three-way reaction. First, there was a reaction from the inner life Christians, including Andrew Murray, Jessie Penn-Lewis, and T. Austin-Sparks. This was the ninth tribe. Second, there was a reaction from evangelical Christians, including C. H. Spurgeon, D. L. Moody, Charles Finney, Hudson Taylor, William Carey, and David Livingstone. This was the tenth tribe. Third, there was a reaction from Pentecostal Christians. This was the eleventh tribe. The twelth tribe is the recovery, which has recovered the New Testament revelation back to the early apostles.

In the recovery the truths from Matthew to Revelation have been recovered by the Lord. In particular, the Lord has recovered the truths concerning the all-inclusive Christ and the New Jerusalem. The truth in the recovery is the consummate truth of the past nineteen centuries. We are standing on the shoulders of all the tribes that have gone before us. Thus, the truth has been extracted, condensed, and crystallized for us.

Let us now consider from chapters eighteen through twenty-two more of the details concerning the allotment of the land.

VI. THE LAND TO BE ALLOTTED
TO THE REST OF THE SEVEN TRIBES

In 18:1 through 19:51 we have the record of the land to be allotted to the rest of the seven tribes. Joshua charged the children of Israel to take possession of the land not yet possessed by them (18:1-3). Then he sent three men from each of the seven tribes to go through the land and write a description of it with a view to it being their inheritance (vv. 4-6, 8-9). After this, Joshua allotted and divided the land unto the seven tribes (v. 10). No land was allotted to the Levites, for the priesthood of Jehovah was their inheritance (v. 7).

A. The Land Allotted to the Tribe of Benjamin

The land allotted to the tribe of Benjamin (vv. 11-28) was between the tribe of Judah and the tribe of Joseph (vv. 11-20).

The land had twenty-six cities with their villages, including Jerusalem (vv. 21-28). Jerusalem was located in the land of Benjamin but was inherited by the children of Judah (15:63).

B. The Land Allotted to the Tribe of Simeon

The land allotted to the tribe of Simeon (19:1-9) was in the midst of the inheritance of the children of Judah (vv. 1, 9) and included seventeen cities with their villages (vv. 2-8).

C. The Land Allotted to the Tribe of Zebulun

The land allotted to the tribe of Zebulun (vv. 10-16) consisted of twelve cities with their villages, including Bethlehem (v. 15).

D. The Land Allotted to the Tribe of Issachar

The land allotted to the tribe of Issachar went from Jezreel to the river Jordan and included sixteen cities with their villages (vv. 17-23).

E. The Land Allotted to the Tribe of Asher

The land allotted to the tribe of Asher went from Helkath to the sea (vv. 24-31). It had twenty-two cities with their villages, including Great Sidon and the fortified city of Tyre (vv. 28-29).

F. The Land Allotted to the Tribe of Naphtali

The land allotted to the tribe of Naphtali (vv. 32-39) was in the midst of Zebulun on the south, Asher on the west, and Judah at the Jordan toward the rising of the sun. This land included nineteen cities with their villages.

G. The Land Allotted to the Tribe of Dan

The land allotted to the tribe of Dan (vv. 40-48) was opposite Japho (v. 46—Joppa, Acts 10:5). When the territory of the children of Dan was lost to them, they went up and fought against Leshem (Laish—Judg. 18:29, at the extreme north of the good land), taking possession of it and naming it according to the name of Dan their father (Josh. 19:47).

H. The Inheritance Given to Joshua

The inheritance given to Joshua (vv. 49-50) was the city of Timnath-serah in the hill country of Ephraim. He asked for this city, and the children of Israel gave it to him according to the commandment of Jehovah.

VII. THE CITIES OF REFUGE

The record in chapter twenty is concerned with the cities of refuge (Exo. 21:13; Num. 35:6a, 10-15).

A. Designated for the Manslayer
Who Killed a Person by Mistake and Unwittingly

Jehovah charged Joshua to tell the children of Israel to designate the cities of refuge so that the manslayer who killed a person by mistake and unwittingly might flee there from the avenger of blood (Josh. 20:1-6).

B. Three in Canaan, West of the Jordan

There were to be three cities of refuge in Canaan, west of the Jordan (v. 7). These cities were Kedesh in Galilee in the hill country of Naphtali, Shechem in the hill country of Ephraim, and Hebron in the hill country of Judah.

C. Three in the Land East of the Jordan

There were to be three other cities of refuge in the land east of the Jordan (vv. 8-9). These cities were Bezer in the wilderness on the plain out of the tribe of Reuben, Ramoth in Gilead out of the tribe of Gad, and Golan in Bashan out of the tribe of Manasseh.

D. Allotted to the Levites

All the cities of refuge were allotted to the Levites (Num. 35:6a).

VIII. THE CITIES WITH THEIR PASTURE LANDS
ALLOTTED TO THE LEVITES,
CLAIMED BY THEM AT SHILOH

The cities with their pasture lands allotted to the Levites were claimed by them at Shiloh. They were given to the

Levites by the children of Israel according to God's command
to Moses (21:1-3). In total, there were forty-eight cities,
including six cities of refuge (v. 41).

A. To the Families of the Kohathites and the Children of Aaron the Priest

To the families of the Kohathites and the children of
Aaron the priest were given thirteen cities from the tribes
of Judah, Simeon, and Benjamin (vv. 4, 8-19).

B. To the Rest of the Children of Kohath

To the rest of the children of Kohath were given ten cities
from the tribes of Ephraim, Dan, and the half-tribe of
Manasseh (vv. 5, 20-26).

C. To the Children of Gershon

To the children of Gershon were given thirteen cities from
the tribes of Issachar, Asher, Naphtali, and the half-tribe of
Manasseh (vv. 6, 27-33).

D. To the Children of Merari

To the children of Merari were given twelve cities from the
tribes of Reuben, Gad, and Zebulun (vv. 7, 34-40).

IX. THE FULFILLMENT OF JEHOVAH'S PROMISE TO THE FATHERS OF ISRAEL THAT HE WOULD GIVE THEM THE GOOD LAND

The allotment of the good land recorded in these chapters
was the fulfillment of Jehovah's promise to the fathers of
Israel that He would give them the good land for their possession and dwelling place (vv. 43-45). Regarding this, verse 45
says, "Not a word failed of all the good things that Jehovah
had spoken to the house of Israel; all came to pass."

X. THE RETURN OF THE TRIBES OF REUBEN, GAD, AND THE HALF-TRIBE OF MANASSEH TO THEIR LAND EAST OF THE JORDAN

Chapter twenty-two gives us an account of the return of

the tribes of Reuben, Gad, and the half-tribe of Manasseh to their land east of the Jordan.

A. Joshua Sending Them with Blessing

Joshua sent them with blessing (vv. 1-9). He called them and said to them that they had kept all that Moses had commanded them and had listened to Joshua's voice in all that he had commanded them, telling them that they had kept the charge of the commandment of Jehovah their God.

B. They Building an Altar
at the River Jordan in the Land of Canaan

When the children of Reuben, the children of Gad, and the half-tribe of Manasseh came into that region of the Jordan that is in the land of Canaan, they built at the river Jordan an altar great in appearance (v. 10).

C. The Children of Israel
Wanting to Go Up in Battle against Them

When the children of Israel heard about the altar that had been built out in front of the land of Canaan, in the region of the Jordan, they wanted to go up in battle against the tribes of Reuben, Gad, and the half-tribe of Manasseh (vv. 11-12). The children of Israel sent Phinehas the priest with ten leaders of the ten tribes of Israel to deal with them (vv. 13-20).

D. The Tribes of Reuben, Gad,
and the Half-tribe of Manasseh
Explaining That the Altar Was Built
Not for Offerings to God but for a Witness

The tribes of Reuben, Gad, and the half-tribe of Manasseh explained to Phinehas and the ten leaders of Israel that they built the altar not for offerings to God but for a witness (vv. 21-29). They claimed that they did not build the altar in rebellion or in trespass against Jehovah (v. 22). They concluded by saying, "Far be it from us that we would rebel against Jehovah and turn away today from following after Jehovah by building an altar for burnt offering, for meal offering, or for sacrifice, besides the altar of Jehovah our God, which is before His tabernacle!" (v. 29).

E. Phinehas the Priest
and the Ten Leaders of Israel
Being Satisfied with Their Explanation

Phinehas the priest and the ten leaders of Israel were satisfied with their explanation and returned to their land (vv. 30-33).

F. They Naming the Altar

The children of Reuben and the children of Gad named the altar, saying that it was a witness that Jehovah is God (v. 34).

LIFE-STUDY OF JOSHUA

MESSAGE THIRTEEN

TEN ASPECTS OF CHRIST

Scripture Reading: Josh. 21:43; 13:33; Deut. 8:7-10

From the first century A.D. to the fifth century, there were many teachings and debates concerning Christology, the study of the person of Christ. The entire Old Testament from Genesis to Malachi is a book on Christology. In the Old Testament there are many types of Christ, and each of these types is related to the study of Christ. The full, complete, and consummate type of Christ is the good land. My burden in this message is to consider ten aspects of the all-inclusive Christ, who is typified by the good land.

CHRIST IN ETERNITY

In eternity Christ was only God, not man. He was the Son of God as the embodiment of God (John 1:18) and the Word of God as the definition of God (v. 1).

IN HIS INCARNATION

One day the eternal Christ came into time, becoming flesh in His incarnation. In His incarnation Christ as the Son of God came "in the likeness of the flesh of sin" (Rom. 8:3). He was not sinful, but by becoming flesh He became something that is related to sin.

Through incarnation the infinite, unlimited, and holy God came out of eternity, and with divinity He entered into time and into the womb of a virgin, remaining there for nine months. Matthew 1:20 indicates that the One who was born into Mary's womb was the very God. First, Christ was born into a human virgin, and then, as a man, He was born out of her. Therefore, Christ is now the God-man; He has not only divinity but also humanity. This reveals that incarnation means that man has been added to God.

Whereas in eternity Christ was merely God, in His incarnation He became the God-man. In Christ as the God-man the human nature and the divine nature have been mingled, blended. However, in this mingling, this blending, the two natures remain distinct, and a third nature is not produced. The divine nature and the human nature remain distinct, yet they are mingled as one. This is Christ in His incarnation.

IN HIS HUMAN LIVING

It is hard for us to imagine that the almighty, unlimited God became an infant lying in a manger. Even in His infancy Christ was a God-man. In a slow, gradual way Christ passed through boyhood into manhood. For thirty years Christ in His humanity lived in a despised country, in the despised town of Nazareth, and in the home of a poor carpenter. Then He came out to teach God, to minister God to people, and to express God's attributes through man's virtues.

This God-man expressed God in man, through man, and with man. Although He was not learned, His speaking was full of wisdom. Although He was humble, He spoke not only with power but also with authority. In every virtue of this One there was something divine, for He was the God-man, God with the divine attributes expressed in man with the human virtues. He was God living as a man, God living a human life.

IN HIS CRUCIFIXION

In His crucifixion Christ died as the Lamb of God to take away man's sin (John 1:29), as the bronze serpent (3:14) to destroy the old serpent, Satan (Heb. 2:14), and as a grain of wheat to release the divine life from within the shell of His humanity (John 12:24). The divine life, which was concealed in His humanity, needed to be released in order to increase and multiply. Therefore, Christ died not only to take away sin and to destroy Satan but also to release the divine life.

By His death on the cross, Christ also terminated the old man and the old creation. Through incarnation Christ became a man, and that man was the old creation. When Christ died, the old man in his totality and ultimate consummation also died. Therefore, when Christ was crucified as a man, the old man was terminated (Rom. 6:6). Furthermore, when Christ became a man, He also became a creature, the Firstborn of all creation (Col. 1:15). This creature was not of the new creation but of the old creation. When Christ was crucified as a creature, the entire old creation was brought to an end.

In addition, in His crucifixion Christ abolished "in His flesh the law of the commandments in ordinances" (Eph. 2:15). The word *ordinances* here refers to rituals, the forms or ways of living and worship, which create enmity and division. Because every nation and culture has its particular ordinances, today there are thousands of different ways of living. Nevertheless, in His crucifixion Christ abolished all these ordinances. Now among us in the church life there is only one way to live—to take Christ as our life, our living, and even our way of living and to live Him.

After the Lord Jesus died, "one of the soldiers pierced His side with a spear, and immediately there came out blood and water" (John 19:34). Blood is for redemption, to deal with sins (Heb. 9:22) for the purchasing of the church (Acts 20:28). Water is for imparting life, for the ministering of God into us as life. The blood of Christ has redeemed us, and the divine life of Christ has flowed into us as a river to minister God into us. Now, as believers in Christ, we have been redeemed back to God, and we have God flowing into us as living water.

Through the crucifixion of Christ, sin has been taken away, Satan has been destroyed, the divine life has been released, the old man has been terminated, the old creation has been brought to an end, the ordinances have been abolished, we have been redeemed back to God, and we have God flowing into us as living water. We all need to have such a view of the crucifixion of Christ.

IN HIS RESURRECTION

In His resurrection Christ became the firstborn Son. Acts 13:33 indicates that resurrection was a birth to the man

Jesus. He was begotten by God in His resurrection to be the firstborn Son of God among many brothers (Rom. 8:29). He was the only begotten Son of God from eternity (John 1:18; 3:16). After incarnation, through resurrection He was begotten by God in His humanity to be God's firstborn Son. We may say that in His resurrection His humanity was "sonized." Furthermore, Christ's resurrection was a birth not only to Him but also to all His millions of believers, who were regenerated by God in the resurrection of Christ (1 Pet. 1:3) to be the many sons of God and the many brothers of Christ (Heb. 2:10-12).

In resurrection Christ also became the life-giving Spirit (1 Cor. 15:45b), compounded with divinity, humanity, death, and resurrection. This Spirit is the consummation of the Triune God and the reality of resurrection. Actually, this Spirit is the pneumatic Christ Himself. According to John 11:25 resurrection is Christ Himself, and Christ is now the life-giving Spirit. Hence, the life-giving Spirit is the reality of resurrection. When we live in this Spirit, we live in resurrection. When we love others in this Spirit, we love them in resurrection.

IN HIS ASCENSION

In His ascension Christ was appointed to be the Lord to possess the whole earth and to be the Christ to bear God's commission to complete God's economy (Acts 2:36; 10:36). He is also the Ruler of the kings of the earth (Rev. 1:5) so that He can be the Savior to save God's chosen people (Acts 5:31).

IN HIS BODY

Christ today is in the Body. In His Body Christ has been enlarged, increased, and multiplied. Originally, the God-man was an individual, but now He is a corporate, universal God-man. Concerning this, 1 Corinthians 12:12 says, "Even as the body is one and has many members, yet all the members of the body, being many, are one body, so also is the Christ." This refers to the corporate Christ, composed of Christ Himself as the Head and the church as His Body with all the believers as members. All the believers of Christ are organically united with Him and constituted with His life and element and have thus become His Body, an organism, to express Him. Hence, He is not only the Head but also the Body.

IN HIS ADVENT

In His advent Christ will come like lightning in the twinkling of an eye (Luke 17:24). We do not have human expressions to describe His coming, but He will be extraordinary to us in His coming.

IN THE MILLENNIAL KINGDOM

In the millennial kingdom Christ, the King, will rule the earth with His overcomers as His co-kings (Rev. 20:4, 6).

IN THE NEW JERUSALEM

In the New Jerusalem Christ will be the holy city. The New Jerusalem will be the consummate manifestation of Christ as the embodiment of the Triune God.

The Christ whom we know, enjoy, possess, and experience is typified by the spacious good land of mountains, rivers, brooks, and plains (Deut. 8:7-10). According to the book of Joshua, this is the Christ not only of the tribes of Judah and Benjamin but also of the tribe of Levi. In the Lord's recovery we are today's Levites. Judah's portion is our portion, and Benjamin's portion also is our portion. This means that we are enjoying all of the experiences of Christ in the twelve tribes, including the early apostles, the church fathers, the martyrs, the reformers, the Protestants, the mystics, the Moravians, the Brethren, the inner life Christians, the evangelicals, and the Pentecostals. This is spoken of in the preface to the Recovery Version:

> Throughout the centuries the understanding of the divine revelation possessed by the saints has always been based upon the light they received, and this understanding has progressed steadily. The consummation of this understanding forms the basis of this translation and its footnotes. Hence, this translation and the accompanying footnotes

could be called the "crystallization" of the understanding of the divine revelation which the saints everywhere have attained to in the past two thousand years. It is our hope that the Recovery Version will carry on the heritage that it has received and will pave the way for future generations.

LIFE-STUDY OF JOSHUA

MESSAGE FOURTEEN

THREE PARTICULAR MATTERS
CONCERNING THE ALLOTMENT OF THE LAND

Scripture Reading: Josh. 17:3-4; 20:1-9; 22:10-34

In this message I have the burden to give a further word on three particular matters concerning the allotment of the good land—the case of the daughters of Zelophehad, the cities of refuge, and the return of the tribes of Reuben, Gad, and the half-tribe of Manasseh to their land east of the Jordan. In typology, these three matters show us certain details regarding the enjoyment of Christ.

THE CASE OF THE DAUGHTERS OF ZELOPHEHAD

Zelophehad, a descendant of Manasseh, had five daughters but no sons (17:3). The daughters claimed the right to inherit their father's inheritance, so that it would remain in his tribe (v. 4; Num. 27:1-11). According to God's ordination, only males had the right of inheritance. Here, however, some females requested an inheritance, and God honored their request.

Having Their Father's Life

The five daughters of Zelophehad had their father's life. This indicates that in order to inherit Christ as our good land, we must have the proper genealogy; that is, we must have the proper origin of life. In the Bible, inheritance is determined according to genealogy. A genealogy is a matter of life, and this life is related to tribes, houses, and families. The fact that the daughters of Zelophehad were of one of the families of Manasseh the son of Joseph indicates that they had the proper origin of life. The enjoyment of Christ as our inheritance depends very much on the life which we have received in Him.

The Father's Family Signifying the Church

Their father's family signifies the church. In the church we have the standing to inherit Christ for our enjoyment. This means that if we would enjoy Christ as our inheritance, participating in His riches, we must have the church life. Our fellowship with the saints in the church life is crucial for our enjoyment of Christ. If we lose our fellowship with the saints, we will lose our enjoyment of Christ. Those who give up the church life with the fellowship of life spontaneously lose their right to inherit the enjoyment of Christ.

The Females Being Weaker Ones

The females signify the weaker ones. In the sight of God, we all are females; we all are weaker ones. Only Christ is the strong One. Spiritually speaking, in the entire universe there is only one male—God embodied in Christ. All the believers, including the brothers, are females. Therefore, the five daughters of Zelophehad typify us.

In particular, the daughters of Zelophehad, being females, signify the weaker ones in the church life. We have been born of God and we are in the church life, having the standing to inherit Christ as our good land for our enjoyment. However, we may be weak, not having the strength or capacity to enjoy Christ. We may have the heart to enjoy Christ but may lack the capacity or the strength to enjoy Him. How, then, can we inherit Christ as the good land? We need to take the way of fellowship, indicated by the contact the daughters of Zelophehad had with their kinsmen. Among the tribe of Manasseh, there were many families with men, signifying the stronger ones. By contacting the stronger kinsmen, the weaker ones were able to keep their father's name and his inheritance within the tribe, signifying the keeping of the enjoyment of Christ. Today, you may be weak, but in God's house, the church, there are stronger ones. Through fellowship, especially in the vital groups, the weaker ones will be strengthened by the stronger ones and thus will be able to enjoy Christ as their inheritance.

THE CITIES OF REFUGE

The cities of refuge (Josh. 20:1-9) were set up by Joshua for those of the children of Israel who unwittingly killed someone. If they would flee to the city of refuge away from the avenger of blood (v. 5), they would be protected. At the death of the high priest, the manslayer would be released to return to his own city (v. 6).

The cities of refuge signify the all-inclusive Christ as the place to which we can escape when we realize that we are sinful. The all-inclusive Christ as the embodiment of the redeeming God is the city of refuge where we are safe-guarded, covered, and concealed. Christ is not only our Savior but also our refuge. Whenever the "storm" of our sin comes, we can run into Christ as our refuge to stay with Him. Then by Christ's death, signified by the death of the high priest, we are released.

THE RETURN OF THE TRIBES
OF REUBEN, GAD, AND THE HALF-TRIBE OF MANASSEH
TO THEIR LAND EAST OF THE JORDAN

Reuben, Gad, and the half-tribe of Manasseh inherited land east of the Jordan (22:9). Moses charged them that they had to fight along with their brothers west of the Jordan before they could enjoy their inheritance east of the Jordan (Num. 32:20-22). After these tribes fought along with their brothers, they were qualified to return to their land to enjoy their inheritance. This indicates that we cannot enjoy Christ without the Body. We must be one with the Body in order to share the inheritance of Christ.

When Reuben, Gad, and the half-tribe of Manasseh returned to enjoy their inheritance of the land, they built a great altar at the river Jordan (Josh. 22:10). This offended the other tribes and caused the children of Israel in Canaan to go up in battle against them (vv. 11-20). Eventually, the tribes of Reuben, Gad, and the half-tribe of Manasseh explained to the other tribes that they built the altar not for offerings but for a witness (vv. 21-29). When Phinehas the priest, the leaders of the assembly, and the heads of the thousands of Israel who

were with him heard this explanation, it seemed good in their
sight (v. 30).

The record in Joshua 22 shows us that no matter what the
situation of God's people might be today, we are not allowed to
set up another altar for the worship of God or for fellowship
with God. In God's economy, among God's people there should
be only one altar, in Jerusalem. All God's people had to go
there to offer their sacrifices to God for their worship and fellowship with God. This indicates that in the enjoyment of
Christ division must be avoided to the uttermost. Nevertheless, in certain places the dissenting ones, not caring for the
one accord in the Lord's recovery, have formed divisions by
building another altar.

It is very significant that in a portion of the holy Word concerned with the inheritance of the good land we have a record
about the building of another altar. This account shows us
that we must avoid division. To enjoy the all-inclusive
Christ as the good land, we must be one people, one Body,
one universal church to testify for Christ.

LIFE-STUDY OF JOSHUA

MESSAGE FIFTEEN

THE DEPARTURE OF JOSHUA

Scripture Reading: Josh. 23—24

In this message we will consider the departure of Joshua described in chapters twenty-three and twenty-four.

At the time of his departure, Joshua had a burden to charge the people of Israel not to forsake God but to remember Him in all His gracious and merciful deeds for them in Egypt, in the wilderness, and in the good land. Joshua told them that if they forsook Jehovah their God, He would no longer dispossess the nations out of their sight. As a result, the nations would become a snare and a trap to the people of Israel (23:13).

Joshua's charge was based upon his more than seventy years' experience with God. When Joshua was young, he was with Moses. During the forty years in the wilderness, Joshua saw what Moses did and learned of him. Then after Moses left, Joshua became the leader of the people of Israel, and he continued as the leader for about twenty-five years. During his years with Moses and his years as leader, Joshua was involved with God's interest. He had learned that God is unique, faithful, and right in everything. He knew that if the Israelites forsook God, they surely would suffer. Therefore, he issued a warning to them, and afterward he died in peace.

Let us now consider the details concerning Joshua's departure recorded in these chapters.

I. JOSHUA'S PARTING WORD TO THE ELDERS, HEADS, JUDGES, AND OFFICERS OF ISRAEL

Chapter twenty-three is Joshua's parting word to the elders, heads, judges, and officers of Israel.

A. Reminding Them
of Jehovah's Faithfulness
in Promising Them and Fighting for Them

Joshua reminded them of Jehovah's faithfulness in promising them the land and in fighting for them. Joshua reminded them that they had seen all that Jehovah their God had done to all the nations because of them (v. 3). Joshua went on to say that he had allotted to them all the nations that remained as an inheritance for their tribes, as well as all the nations that he had cut off (v. 4). Then Joshua said, "Jehovah your God, He will thrust them out before you and dispossess them out of your sight; and you will possess their land, as Jehovah your God spoke to you" (v. 5).

B. Encouraging Them to Love
Jehovah Their God and to Cling to Him

Next, Joshua encouraged the elders, heads, judges, and officers of Israel to love Jehovah their God and to cling to Him (vv. 6-11). He charged them to be strong to keep and do all that is written in the book of the law of Moses, not going unto the nations that remained with them and not making mention of the names of their gods, nor serving them, nor bowing down to them (vv. 6-7). Rather, the people of Israel were to cling to Jehovah their God, for He had dispossessed great and strong nations because of them. After speaking about this, Joshua said, "Be very careful therefore for yourselves, that you love Jehovah your God" (v. 11).

C. Warning Them with the Snare,
the Trap, the Scourge in Their Sides,
and Thorns in Their Eyes

Joshua continued by warning them not to turn back and cling to the remainder of the nations, not to marry into them, and not to go among them (v. 12). Then Joshua charged them, saying, "Know for certain that Jehovah your God will no longer dispossess these nations out of your sight, but they will become a snare and a trap to you, and a scourge in your sides and thorns in your eyes, until you perish from this good land that Jehovah your God has given you" (v. 13). Joshua went on to remind them that they knew in their hearts and souls that not a word had failed of all the good things that Jehovah had spoken concerning them. All had come to pass for them. However, if they forsook Jehovah their God, just as the good things had come upon them, so would Jehovah cause all the evil things to come upon them, until He destroyed them from the good land that He had given them (vv. 14-15). If they transgressed the covenant of Jehovah and served other gods, the anger of Jehovah would burn against them, and they would perish quickly from the good land (v. 16).

II. JOSHUA'S PARTING WORD
TO ALL THE TRIBES OF ISRAEL WITH THEIR ELDERS, HEADS, JUDGES, AND OFFICERS

Chapter twenty-four is Joshua's parting word to all the tribes of Israel with their elders, heads, judges, and officers.

A. Reminding Them of Jehovah Their God's Marvelous Deeds to Their Forefathers and to Themselves

Joshua reminded them of Jehovah their God's marvelous deeds to their forefathers Abraham, Isaac, and Jacob and to themselves in Egypt, in the wilderness, and in Canaan the good land (vv. 1-13).

B. Charging Them to Fear Jehovah and Serve Him in Sincerity and Faithfulness

In his parting word to all the tribes, Joshua also charged them to fear Jehovah and serve Him in sincerity and faithfulness and to put away the gods whom their fathers served across the River and in Egypt (v. 14). Joshua told them that if it seemed wrong in their sight to serve Jehovah, they should choose for themselves whom they would serve—the gods from across the River or the gods of the Amorites. Then Joshua assured them that he and his house would serve Jehovah (v. 15).

C. The People Answering That They Would Not Forsake Jehovah to Serve Other Gods

The people answered that they would not forsake Jehovah to serve other gods (vv. 16-18). They claimed that, since Jehovah had brought them out of the land of Egypt, had done great things in their sight and had preserved them, and had driven out all the peoples from before them, they would serve Jehovah, for He was their God.

D. Warning Them That Jehovah Would Do Them Harm and Consume Them If They Forsook Him and Served Other Gods

Joshua warned them that Jehovah would do them harm and consume them if they forsook Him and served other gods (vv. 19-20). Then he charged them to put away the foreign gods that were among them and to incline their hearts to Jehovah, the God of Israel (v. 23).

E. Making a Covenant for the People of Israel in Shechem

Finally, Joshua made a covenant for the people of Israel in Shechem. He also made a statute and an ordinance for them, taking a great stone and erecting it there under the terebinth that was at the sanctuary of Jehovah to be a witness against Israel, lest they act deceptively against their God (vv. 25-27).

III. THE DEATH AND BURIAL OF JOSHUA

Joshua died at the age of one hundred and ten years, and they buried him in the territory of his inheritance, in Timnath-serah in the hill country of Ephraim (vv. 29-30).

IV. ISRAEL SERVING JEHOVAH THROUGHOUT ALL THE DAYS OF JOSHUA AND ALL THE DAYS OF THE ELDERS AFTER JOSHUA

Israel served Jehovah throughout all the days of Joshua and throughout all the days of the elders whose days extended after Joshua's and who knew all the work of Jehovah that He had done for Israel (v. 31).

V. JOSEPH'S BONES BEING BURIED IN SHECHEM

Joseph's bones, which the children of Israel had brought up from Egypt, were buried in Shechem (v. 32). They were buried in the portion of the field that Jacob had bought from the children of Hamor the father of Shechem (Gen. 33:18-19), which became the inheritance of the children of Joseph.

VI. THE DEATH AND BURIAL
OF ELEAZAR THE SON OF AARON

The book of Joshua concludes with a word concerning the death and burial of Eleazar the son of Aaron (24:33). Eleazar was buried in the hill of Phinehas his son, which had been given to him in the hill country of Ephraim.

LIFE-STUDY OF JUDGES

MESSAGE ONE

AN INTRODUCTORY WORD

Scripture Reading: Judg. 1:1-2; 2:11—3:11; 21:25; Acts 13:19-20

As we begin the life-study of Judges, I have the burden to speak a word concerning the intrinsic significance of this book.

In order to understand the history in the Old Testament, we need the full scope of the Scriptures. If we read the Old Testament according to this full scope, we will realize that at Mount Sinai God married Israel. In His concept and desire, He wanted to be to Israel as a husband to a wife, and He expected Israel to act as a wife toward Him. We need to keep this point in mind as we read the book of Judges.

In writing the books of history, Samuel put Judges after Joshua to show us what kind of life Israel lived toward her Husband. For some reason, she did not have a heart to be the wife of Jehovah. As a wife, she forgot her Husband, left her Husband, and acted according to her own desires. Eventually, Israel became a harlot. At the time of Hosea, Israel was a harlot in the eyes of God (Hosea 1:2; 2:2). Having fallen into the sin of adultery, she did not have a definite husband. In addition to Jehovah as her Husband, she had many other men. This was the situation of Israel in the book of Judges. In the book of Judges there is a terrible picture of a wife forsaking her Husband and not even acknowledging His existence. This is an ugly picture of a harlot, a wife who forsook her Husband and went after idols.

In the beginning Israel had a bridal love toward God, but after her marriage she lost her position as a chaste wife to her husband. She forsook God and went to idols. Every idol was a "man," and Israel became full of idols. Jeremiah 11:13

says that according to the number of the streets of Jerusalem the people had set up altars to burn incense to their idols. Ezekiel 16:24 tells us that Israel made "a high place in every street." This means that there was an idol on every street. This corresponds to the New Testament, which shows us another great harlot in Revelation 17, the Roman Catholic Church, which is the mother of many harlots. Since the mother of the harlots is the apostate Roman Church, the harlots, the daughters of the apostate church, must be all the sects and groups in Christianity that hold to some extent the teachings, practices, and traditions of the apostate Roman Church.

In the book of Judges, a particular saying is repeated a number of times: "In those days there was no king in Israel; everyone did that which was right in his own eyes" (17:6; 18:1; 19:1; 21:25). But God was the King! According to the principle in the Bible, the husband is the head of the marriage and the head of the family. In creation God ordained that the man would have this authority; therefore, he also has the kingship. In typology and in figure, God is the unique man. We all are females because we, the church, are the corporate wife to Christ. Since God is our Creator and our Lord, He should also be our King.

When Israel said that there was no king among them, this meant that they had annulled God and His status. In the book of 1 Samuel, the children of Israel asked God to appoint a king for them (8:5). This was a great offense to God (v. 7). Even though Israel was a wife to God, she became a harlot. She did not recognize God's kingship, and she did not recognize God as her Husband. Therefore, the children of Israel did what was right in their own eyes, and as a result they became rotten and corrupted.

This is what we see in the book of Judges. The history in this book is thus a history of rottenness. After the story of Judah and Caleb in 1:1-20, Israel's history as recorded in Judges was full of the rottenness and corruption of a harlot. This is the intrinsic significance of the book of Judges.

I would now like to give a brief introductory word to our study of Judges.

I. JOSHUA BEING THE BOOK OF ISRAEL'S HISTORY FULL OF MARVELOUS VICTORIES AND JUDGES BEING THE BOOK OF ISRAEL'S HISTORY FULL OF MISERABLE DEFEATS

We need to see the contrast between the books of Joshua and Judges. Joshua is the book of Israel's history full of the marvelous victories over the inhabitants of Canaan in the presence of Jehovah. Judges, on the contrary, is the book of Israel's history full of miserable defeats under their enemies in the forsaking of Jehovah.

II. THE WRITER

The writer of the book of Judges probably was Samuel. Many expositors of the Scriptures hold this view.

III. THE TIME

The time covered in Judges comprises about 305 years, from about 1425 B.C. (after Joshua's death—1:1) to 1120 B.C. (at the death of Samson—16:30-31; cf. Acts 13:19-20). The following list is the chronological sequence according to history:

1.	2:6-9	about	1426 B.C.
2.	1:1-36	"	1425 B.C.
3.	2:1-5	"	1425 B.C.
4.	2:10-13		
5.	Chs. 17—21	"	1406 B.C.
	(Ruth	"	1322-1312 B.C.)
6.	2:14—16:31	"	? -1120 B.C.

IV. THE PLACE

The place of Judges was Canaan.

V. THE CONTENT

The content of Judges consists of the children of Israel trusting in God, forsaking God, being defeated by their enemies, being delivered through the judges, and becoming corrupted (1:1-2; 2:11—3:11). When the children of Israel, who had trusted in God, forsook God, they were defeated by their enemies. Because of their miserable situation, they repented, and the Lord mercifully raised up judges to deliver them. However, after the children of Israel were delivered, they became corrupted. All this became a cycle that was repeated over and over in Judges.

VI. THE CENTRAL THOUGHT

The central thought of the book of Judges is that Israel forsook God, suffered defeat by their enemies, and became rotten; and since there was no king among them, everyone did that which was right in his own eyes (17:6; 18:1; 19:1; 21:25).

VII. THE SECTIONS

The book of Judges has three sections: Israel's trusting in God (1:1—2:5); Israel's forsaking of God (comprising their suffering of defeats, their repentance, and God's deliverance (2:6—16:31); and Israel's becoming corrupted (17:1—21:25).

LIFE-STUDY OF JUDGES

MESSAGE TWO

THE BEAUTIFUL SCENE OF ISRAEL'S TRUSTING IN GOD

Scripture Reading: Judg. 1

In this message we will consider chapter one of Judges. This chapter describes the beautiful scene of Israel's trusting in God.

I. JUDAH'S BOLDNESS AND VICTORY

In verses 1 through 21 we see Judah's boldness and victory.

A. Inquiring of Jehovah and Jehovah's Answer and Promise

After the death of Joshua, the children of Israel inquired of Jehovah concerning who would go up for them first against the Canaanites in order to fight against them (v. 1). Jehovah gave His answer and promise, saying, "Judah shall go up. Behold, I have given the land into his hand" (v. 2). This marvelous picture of oneness with the Lord, of the organic union of God with His people, is a continuation of the oneness in the book of Joshua when the people of Israel first entered into the good land.

B. Judah and Simeon His Brother's Coordination

"Judah said to Simeon his brother, Come up with me into my lot, and we will fight against the Canaanites; and I will also go with you into your lot. And Simeon went with him" (v. 3). Here we see a wonderful coordination between two tribes—Judah, the strongest tribe, and Simeon, a weak tribe.

C. Judah Going Up, and Jehovah Giving the Canaanites and the Perizzites into Their Hand

According to verses 4 through 10, Judah went up, and

Jehovah gave the Canaanites and the Perizzites into their hand, and they struck ten thousand of them in Bezek. Then the children of Judah fought against Jerusalem and took it, striking it with the edge of the sword and setting it on fire. Afterward they went down to fight against the Canaanites who inhabited the hill country and the southland and the lowland.

D. Caleb's Victory over Hebron through His Son-in-law Othniel

This chapter also speaks of Caleb's victory over Hebron through his son-in-law Othniel (vv. 11-15, 20). The name *Othniel* means "lion of God." Caleb said that to whoever struck Kiriath-sepher and took it he would give Achsah his daughter as wife. Othniel took Kiriath-sepher, and Caleb gave him Achsah as wife. She spoke to her father, saying, "Give me a blessing, for you have given me the southland; give me also springs of water" (v. 15a). So Caleb gave her the upper springs and the lower springs. Verse 20 tells us that Hebron was given to Caleb, as Moses had spoken, and that Caleb dispossessed the three sons of Anak from there.

E. Judah Fighting, with Simeon His Brother, and Utterly Destroying the Canaanites

Judah fought, with Simeon his brother, and utterly destroyed the Canaanites, and Jehovah was with Judah. They took possession of the hill country, but they were not able to dispossess the inhabitants of the valley, for they had chariots of iron (vv. 16-19).

F. The Children of Benjamin Not Dispossessing the Jebusites

The children of Benjamin did not dispossess the Jebusites, who dwelt in Jerusalem. Rather, the Jebusites continued to dwell with the children of Benjamin in Jerusalem (v. 21). This indicates that even though Judah was bold and victorious, his victory was not absolute, for there was a shortage in not dispossessing the inhabitants of the valley and in not dispossessing the Jebusites.

II. THE HOUSE OF JOSEPH
GOING UP TO FIGHT AGAINST BETHEL

The house of Joseph went up to fight against Bethel, and Jehovah was with them. First, they spied out Bethel. When those who watched saw a man coming out of the city, they told him that if he showed them the entrance of the city, they would be merciful to him. He showed them the entrance, and they struck the people of the city with their sword, but they let the man and all his family go (vv. 22-26).

III. SOME DEFECTS

Although this chapter portrays the beautiful scene of Israel's trusting in God, this chapter nevertheless describes some defects (vv. 27-36).

A. Manasseh, Ephraim, Zebulun, Asher, and Naphtali
Not Dispossessing the Canaanites

When Israel became strong, they made the Canaanites forced labor, but they did not utterly dispossess them (v. 28). Manasseh, Ephraim, Zebulun, Asher, and Naphtali did not dispossess the Canaanites, who persisted in dwelling in their lands and became forced labor (vv. 27, 29-33).

B. The Amorites Pushing
the Children of Dan into the Hill Country

The Amorites pushed the children of Dan into the hill country, not allowing them to come down into the valley. The Amorites persisted in dwelling with them, but the house of Joseph prevailed so that they became forced labor (vv. 34-36).

LIFE-STUDY OF JUDGES

MESSAGE THREE

THE MISERABLE HISTORY
OF ISRAEL'S FORSAKING OF GOD

CHAPTERS 2—16

(1)

Scripture Reading: Judg. 2:1—3:6

In this message we will consider 2:1—3:6. Before we come to these verses, I would like to say a word concerning the intrinsic significance of this portion of the Word.

We have seen that at Mount Sinai God entered into a marriage union with Israel and that He wanted her to remain in the most intimate contact with Him in this marvelous marriage union. But Israel rejected God as her Husband and as her King and "went about as harlots after other gods and worshipped them" (2:17). In dealing with this situation, the King became a servant, as the Angel of Jehovah, to admonish the children of Israel (vv. 1-5).

The Angel of Jehovah is spoken of throughout the Old Testament, from Exodus 3 through Zechariah 3. The Angel of Jehovah is also mentioned in Judges 2 and 6. The word *angel* is capitalized in these instances because this Angel is a particular Angel. The Angel of Jehovah is just God Himself in His Divine Trinity serving His elect as a Servant.

When Moses was being called by God to lead Israel out of Egypt, the calling Jehovah became the Angel of Jehovah. In Exodus 3 the names *Jehovah* and *the Angel of Jehovah* are used interchangeably (vv. 2, 4). The embodiment of the Triune God is Christ, and Christ is the Angel of Jehovah, who took care of Israel as the acting Jehovah in the Old Testament. Christ is the acting God, not a silent, passive God. For Christ to be the Angel of Jehovah means that God has appointed and commissioned Himself in His Divine Trinity to act in caring for His people.

Because Israel did not act as a proper wife, the very Jehovah who was the Husband, the Head, and the King of Israel became a Servant to His wife. This means that He did not come to her as a Husband, Head, or King but came to her as the Angel of Jehovah, who was sent by Jehovah (Zech. 2:9-11). Since Israel did not consider Jehovah as the Head, He became a Servant to serve her. His admonition in Judges 2 was the admonition of a servant.

With respect to Christ as the Angel of Jehovah, let us review what is revealed concerning Christ in the four Gospels. In the Gospel of Matthew Christ is presented as the King, and in the Gospel of Mark the King is presented as a Slave. The King-Savior thus became a Slave-Savior. In the Gospel of Luke the Slave-Savior is presented as a Man-Savior in His human virtues with the divine attributes. However, He is more than just a man; He is also God. Therefore, in the Gospel of John He is presented as God (1:1). He is the eternal God who became flesh (v. 14). Our Savior, therefore, is a God-man, who is both a King and a Slave. This is the intrinsic significance of the four Gospels.

Our God wants to save us and be our King, and we need to acknowledge Him as our Head and King. In order to save us, however, the King had to become a Servant and a Slave. As a Slave He is both God and man. He is a man, but His substance, His very essence, is God.

In His divinity God is our King and Head. Because our situation was so poor, the King had to become a Servant to serve us. The Servant sent by God in Judges 2 was actually Jehovah Himself in His acting situation. He did not come to rebuke or command; rather, He came to admonish and to take care of Israel. This is the significance of the Angel of Jehovah in Judges 2.

Having seen the intrinsic significance of 2:1—3:6, let us now consider this portion in some detail.

I. THE ADMONITION OF THE ANGEL OF JEHOVAH

In 2:1-5 we have the admonition of the Angel of Jehovah,

who, as we have seen, is Christ as the acting Jehovah in the Old Testament taking care of Israel (Exo. 3:2-10; 14:19; Judg. 6:21).

A. Reminding Israel

In verses 1 and 2a the Angel of Jehovah reminded Israel of three matters. First, He reminded them of Jehovah's delivering them out from Egypt and His bringing them into the promised land (v. 1a). Second, He reminded them of Jehovah's faithfulness in keeping His promise to them (v. 1b). Third, He reminded them of Jehovah's charge to them that they should not make a covenant with the inhabitants of Canaan and that they should tear down their altars (v. 2a).

B. Warning Israel

In verses 2b and 3 the Angel of Jehovah gave a warning to Israel. First, He told them that they had not listened to His voice, and then He asked them concerning what they had done (v. 2b). Because Israel did not listen to Him, He went on to say that He would not drive the Canaanites out from before them, but they would be like thorns in Israel's sides, and the gods of the Canaanites would be a snare to Israel (v. 3).

C. Israel's Reaction to the Words of the Angel of Jehovah

Verse 4 tells us Israel's reaction to the words of the Angel of Jehovah. The people lifted up their voice and wept. Thus, they called the name of that place Bochim, and there they offered to Jehovah (v. 5).

II. THE REASON FOR ISRAEL'S FORSAKING OF GOD

In verses 6 through 10 we see the reason for Israel's forsaking of God.

A. Because of the Death of Joshua, of the Elders, and of the Generation Who Saw All the Great Work of Jehovah That He Had Done for Israel

When Joshua sent the people away, each of the children of Israel went to his own inheritance. The people served

Jehovah throughout all the days of Joshua and throughout all the days of the elders whose days extended after Joshua and who saw all the great work of Jehovah that He had done for Israel. Eventually, all that generation died. The death of Joshua, of the elders, and of that entire generation was the reason for Israel's forsaking of God (vv. 6-10a).

B. Because the Present Generation Did Not Know Jehovah or the Work That He Had Done for Israel

Also, "another generation," the present generation, who did not know Jehovah or the work that He had done for Israel, rose up after them (v. 10b).

III. THE CYCLE OF THE MISERABLE HISTORY OF ISRAEL'S FORSAKING OF GOD

Verses 11 through 20 are a record of the cycle of the miserable history of Israel's forsaking of God.

A. Israel's Forsaking of Jehovah and Turning to the Idols of the Canaanites

The children of Israel did what was evil in the sight of Jehovah, serving the idols of the Canaanites (vv. 11-13). They forsook Jehovah, the God of their fathers, who brought them out of the land of Egypt, and they followed after other gods from among the gods of the peoples who surrounded them.

B. Jehovah's Anger Burning against Israel

The anger of Jehovah burned against Israel, and He delivered them into the hands of plunderers and sold them into the hand of their enemies around them (vv. 14-15). Whenever the children of Israel went out, the hand of Jehovah was against them for evil.

C. Israel's Groaning and Jehovah's Pity on Them in Raising Up Judges to Save Them from the Hand of Their Enemies

Israel groaned because of those who oppressed them and crushed them, and Jehovah was moved to pity and raised

up judges to save them from the hand of their enemies
(vv. 16-18).

D. After the Death of the Judge,
Israel Turning and Acting More Corruptly
by Following After Other Gods

When the judge raised up by Jehovah died, the people of
Israel turned and acted more corruptly than their fathers by
following after other gods in order to serve them and worship
them. They did not cease from any of their practices or from
their stubborn way (v. 19).

E. The Anger of Jehovah
Burning Again against Israel

When the people turned and acted more corruptly, the
anger of Jehovah burned again against Israel (v. 20).

IV. JEHOVAH'S TESTING OF ISRAEL

In 2:21—3:6 we have Jehovah's testing of Israel.

A. By the Nations
Who Were Left after Joshua's Death

Jehovah tested Israel by the nations who were left after
Joshua's death (2:21—3:4). Because Israel transgressed
Jehovah's covenant and did not listen to His voice, Jehovah
said that He would no longer dispossess from before them any
of the nations that Joshua left when he died. His purpose in
not dispossessing the nations was to test Israel through them
as to whether they would keep the way of Jehovah by walking
in it, as their fathers kept it. Thus, these nations "were for the
testing of Israel, to know whether they would listen to the
commandments of Jehovah, which He commanded their
fathers through Moses" (3:4).

B. By Israel's Failure

According to verses 5 and 6, Israel failed in three matters:
in dwelling among the Canaanites (v. 5); in taking the
daughters of the Canaanites as their wives and giving their

own daughters to the sons of the Canaanites (v. 6a); and in serving the gods of the Canaanites (v. 6b).

LIFE-STUDY OF JUDGES

MESSAGE FOUR

THE MISERABLE HISTORY
OF ISRAEL'S FORSAKING OF GOD
CHAPTERS 2—16

(2)

THE FIRST THREE CYCLES
OF THE MISERABLE HISTORY OF ISRAEL

Scripture Reading: Judg. 3:7—5:31

Before we come to 3:7—5:31, I have the burden to speak
a word concerning the intrinsic significance of this portion
of Judges.

Prior to the history recorded in these chapters, the people
of Israel had never had a female leader. Then, suddenly, God
raised up a female, Deborah, as a judge of Israel. Regarding
this, we need to realize that in the Bible, whenever God does
something which stands out as being extraordinary, it is very
significant. It indicates, first, man's failure, and then, God's
excellent act. At the time of Judges 4, all the men of Israel
had failed, so God raised up a woman. That raising up of a
female changed the entire condition of Israel.

In the Bible a proper female indicates one who is in
submission to God, one who keeps God's ordination. This is
the position that Israel should have taken before God, but the
situation in Israel had become fully abnormal. The men had
left their position before Jehovah. Hence, Israel violated
God's ordination, leaving her position as God's wife and forsaking Him for hundreds of idols. This brought Israel into a
miserable situation and condition.

According to God's creation, Deborah was a very capable
person. By reading her song in chapter five, we can see that
she was full of ability, capacity, insight, and foresight. But

such an excellent person was very submissive. God made her the leader, yet she kept the proper order and took Barak as her covering (4:6-9). She realized that she needed a man to be her covering. Actually, Barak did nearly nothing, yet Deborah took him as her "head covering." When she took this kind of standing, the whole nation became different. In their miserable situation no one would take the lead to fight for Jehovah's interest, and no one would be willing to follow. But when this excellent, extraordinary woman took the lead to practice the female submission to the man, the entire country came into the proper order. Everyone returned to his or her proper position. Thus Deborah could say in her song, "Then a remnant of the nobles went down; / The people of Jehovah went down with me against the mighty" (5:13). All the leaders took the lead, and all the people followed; the army was formed. At first, only some of the people followed, but eventually they all followed. From this we see that the entire country came into an excellent order, assuming the proper position before Jehovah.

Judges 5:15-16 speaks of "great resolutions in heart" and "great searchings of heart." In Israel's miserable situation, no one was searching his heart. But the people needed a great searching of their hearts, and they needed to make great resolutions in their hearts to rise up and follow the others to fight for God's kingdom.

We may apply this to our practice of the vital groups today. For the vital groups we need much prayer with repentance. In our prayer spontaneously the searching of the heart comes to us. This issues in a resolve to live for the Lord and to fight for the Lord according to the present need in His recovery. In particular, we need to make a resolution before the Lord concerning gaining persons for His increase. This is "great resolutions in heart."

Judges 3:12-13 says that Jehovah strengthened Israel's enemies, but 4:6-16 reveals that Jehovah was fighting for Israel. This shows that God is a God of incarnation. God wants man to match Him so that He can move. If Israel had not fought, God would not have fought for them. However, because Israel did fight under Deborah in a proper order, God fought for them. The principle is the same with us today. If we do not go out to gain sinners, God will not go, but if we go, God also will go. However, this kind of going out needs a searching of our heart and a resolution in our heart. God will not work until we become active in this searching of our heart and making resolutions in our heart. This is the way to fight the battle; this is the way to preach the gospel; and this is the way to gain sinners to become members of Christ.

Judges 5:31b says, "May those who love Him be like the sun / When it rises in its might." For the sun to rise in its might means that it shines brightly, brilliantly, and gloriously. We need the searchings, the resolutions, and the rising up to shine like the sun. If all the churches would be like this, they surely would enjoy the victory. May all the dear saints in the Lord's recovery have great searchings and make great resolutions, and may they all, by loving the Lord, rise up like the sun to shine brightly.

Let us now consider the first three cycles of the miserable history of Israel in 3:7—5:31.

I. THE FIRST CYCLE

The record of the first cycle is given in 3:7-11a.

A. Israel's Evil in Forsaking Jehovah

The children of Israel did evil in forsaking Jehovah to serve the Baalim and the Asheroth (v. 7).

B. Jehovah's Anger Burning against Israel

Because Israel did what was evil in the sight of Jehovah, His anger burned against them (v. 8a).

C. Jehovah Selling Israel into the Hand of the King of Mesopotamia

Jehovah sold Israel into the hand of Cushan-rishathaim, king of Mesopotamia, and Israel served him eight years (v. 8b).

D. Israel Crying Out to Jehovah

The children of Israel cried out to Jehovah (v. 9a).

E. Jehovah Raising Up a Savior

Jehovah raised up a savior, Othniel the son of Caleb's younger brother. The Spirit of Jehovah came upon him, and he saved Israel from Cushan-rishathaim (vv. 9b-10).

F. The Land Having Rest Forty Years

The end of the first cycle was that the land had rest forty years (v. 11a).

II. THE SECOND CYCLE

In 3:11b-31 we have the second cycle of Israel's miserable history.

A. Othniel, the Judge, Dying

In verse 11b we are told that Othniel, the judge, died.

B. Israel Again Doing That Which Was Evil in the Sight of Jehovah

After the death of Othniel, the children of Israel again did that which was evil in the sight of Jehovah (v. 12a).

C. Jehovah Strengthening Eglon King of Moab against Israel

Because Israel did that which was evil in His sight, Jehovah strengthened Eglon king of Moab against Israel. Eglon gathered the children of Ammon and Amalek to himself and went and struck Israel, taking possession of the city of palms (vv. 12b-13).

D. Israel Serving Eglon King of Moab Eighteen Years

Israel served Eglon king of Moab eighteen years (v. 14).

E. Israel Crying to Jehovah, and Jehovah Raising Up a Savior for Them

Israel cried to Jehovah, and Jehovah raised up a savior for them, Ehud the son of Gera, the Benjaminite (v. 15a).

F. Ehud Killing Eglon King of Moab
and Defeating the Moabites

Ehud killed Eglon king of Moab by a scheme, and then he defeated the Moabites with the children of Israel from the hill country of Ephraim, killing about ten thousand Moabites (vv. 15b-29).

G. Moab Being Subdued by Israel,
and the Land Having Rest Eighty Years

Moab was subdued that day by Israel, and the land had rest eighty years (v. 30).

H. Shamgar the Son of Anath Also Saving Israel

After Ehud there was Shamgar the son of Anath, who struck six hundred Philistines with an ox goad. He also saved Israel (v. 31).

III. THE THIRD CYCLE

Chapters four and five are a record of the third cycle.

A. Israel Again Doing That Which Was Evil
in the Sight of Jehovah after Ehud Died

The children of Israel again did that which was evil in the sight of Jehovah after Ehud died (4:1).

B. Jehovah Selling Israel
into the Hand of Jabin King of Canaan

Jehovah sold Israel into the hand of Jabin king of Canaan, the captain of whose army was Sisera. He had nine hundred iron chariots, and he oppressed Israel severely for twenty years (vv. 2, 3b).

C. Israel Crying Out to Jehovah

The children of Israel cried out to Jehovah (v. 3a).

D. Deborah, a Prophetess,
Being Raised Up as a Judge of Israel

Deborah, a prophetess, was raised up as a judge of Israel.

She would sit under the palm of Deborah, and the children of Israel went up to her for judgment (vv. 4-5).

E. Deborah, with Barak
and the Children of Naphtali and Zebulun,
Defeating Jabin King of Canaan

Deborah, with Barak and the children of Naphtali and Zebulun, defeated Jabin the king of Canaan and the captain of his army, Sisera, through Jehovah's fighting for them (vv. 6-16). Verse 15a says, "Jehovah threw Sisera and all his chariots and all his camp into confusion with the edge of the sword before Barak."

F. Sisera, the Captain of King Jabin's Army,
Being Killed by Jael

In verse 9 Deborah prophesied that Jehovah would sell Sisera into the hand of a woman. In verses 17 through 22 Sisera, the captain of King Jabin's army, was killed by Jael, the wife of Heber the Kenite, as Deborah had predicted.

G. God Subduing Jabin King of Canaan
before the Children of Israel

God subdued Jabin king of Canaan before the children of Israel. They prevailed more and more against Jabin until they destroyed him (vv. 23-24).

H. The Song of Deborah and Barak

Judges 5:1-31a is the song of Deborah and Barak.

1. Celebrating Triumphantly Their Victory
over Jabin King of Canaan

Verses 4 and 5 say, "O Jehovah, when You went forth from Seir, / When You marched from the field of Edom; / The earth trembled, the heavens also dripped, / Indeed the clouds dripped water. / The mountains quaked at the presence of Jehovah, / Sinai there, at the presence of Jehovah, the God of Israel." Here Deborah and Barak celebrated triumphantly their victory over Jabin king of Canaan, given to them by God.

2. Appreciating the Leaders of Israel Who Took the Lead and the People of Israel Who Willingly Offered Themselves

Deborah and Barak appreciated the leaders of Israel who took the lead and the people of Israel who willingly offered themselves, some of whom had great resolutions in their heart and great searchings of their heart (vv. 2, 9, 13-18).

3. Praising the Stars That Fought with Sisera from Heaven, from Their Courses

The song of Deborah and Barak also praises the stars that fought with Sisera from heaven, from their courses, and the ancient river Kishon that swept away the kings of Canaan (vv. 20-21).

4. Praising the Angel of Jehovah, Christ, Who Took Care of Their Battle

"Curse Meroz, says the Angel of Jehovah; / Bitterly curse its inhabitants. / For they did not come to the aid of Jehovah, / To the aid of Jehovah against the mighty" (v. 23). Here the song praises the Angel of Jehovah, Christ, who took care of their battle.

5. Blessing Jael, the Wife of Heber the Kenite

In verses 24 through 27 the song of Deborah and Barak blesses Jael, the wife of Heber the Kenite, who killed Sisera, the captain of the army of Jabin, king of Canaan. Verse 24 says, "Blessed among women shall Jael be, / The wife of Heber the Kenite; / Blessed among the women in the tent shall she be."

6. Mocking Ironically the Imagination of the Mother of Sisera concerning Her Son's Good Fortune

Verses 28 through 30 continue by mocking ironically the imagination of the mother of Sisera concerning her son's good fortune.

7. *Blessing Israel*

Verse 31a is a blessing upon Israel: "May all your enemies so perish, O Jehovah. / But may those who love Him be like the sun / When it rises in its might."

I. The Land Having Rest Forty Years

Chapter five concludes by saying that the land had rest forty years (v. 31b).

LIFE-STUDY OF JUDGES

MESSAGE FIVE

THE MISERABLE HISTORY
OF ISRAEL'S FORSAKING OF GOD
CHAPTERS 2—16

(3)

THE FOURTH CYCLE
OF ISRAEL'S MISERABLE HISTORY

Scripture Reading: Judg. 6:1—8:32

After considering 6:1—8:32 before the Lord, I believe that the way to present the intrinsic significance of this portion of Judges is to present, first, the secret of Gideon's success and then the secret of his failure.

Gideon, a marvelous judge who was called by Jehovah in a very particular way, was successful because of four things. First, he listened carefully to the word of God, something that was rare among the children of Israel at that time. Second, Gideon obeyed God's word and acted on it. Third, he tore down the altar of Baal and cut down the Asherah (6:25-28). This touched God's heart. In the degradation of Israel, God hated the idols to the uttermost. God as the genuine Husband regarded all the idols as men with whom His wife Israel had committed harlotry. Fourth, by tearing down the altar of Baal and cutting down the Asherah that belonged to his father, Gideon sacrificed his relationship with his father and his enjoyment of society. Because of what he had done, the men of the city of Ophrah contended with him and even wanted to kill him (vv. 28-30). For Gideon to do such a thing for God required that he sacrifice his own interests, and his sacrifice was a strong factor of his success.

The selection of the three hundred in 7:2-7 also stresses the sacrifice of our personal interests and enjoyment for

God's purpose. When Gideon blew the trumpet to call the people to fight against the Midianites, thirty-two thousand responded. God said that those who were with Gideon were too many for God to deliver Midian into their hand, for Israel might have vaunted himself against God, saying, "My own hand has saved me" (v. 2). By telling Gideon that he had too many people, God was indicating that He would fight for them. First, twenty-two thousand went home because they were afraid (v. 3). Then Jehovah tested the remaining ten thousand by bringing them to the water to drink. Those who bowed down on their knees and lapped as a dog laps were sent home (v. 5). Only the three hundred who lapped the water into their mouths with their hands were chosen by God for the battle against Midian (v. 6). Jehovah told Gideon that through the three hundred men who lapped in that way, He would save them from Midian. Like Gideon, these three hundred were willing to sacrifice in order to be used by God.

As a result of these four factors, Gideon received a reward: the economical Spirit came upon him (6:34). Hence, he became powerful and with only three hundred men defeated two princes and two kings (7:25; 8:10-12). With Gideon we have a picture of a man in union with God, a God-man, to fulfill God's word and to carry out God's economy.

After his great success—the greatest success in all the cycles of Israel's history recorded in Judges—Gideon had a terrible failure. The secret of his failure comprises three factors. First, Gideon was not kind. He killed those country-men who did not support him (vv. 16-17), breaking the sixth commandment of God (Exo. 20:13). Second, he indulged in the lust of the flesh, not exercising any restriction over his fleshly lust. This is indicated by Judges 8:30, which tells us that Gideon had seventy sons, "for he had many wives." In addition, his concubine who was in Shechem also bore him a son (v. 31). By this Gideon broke the seventh commandment (Exo. 20:14). Third, although he did a good thing in refusing to rule over the people (Judg. 8:22-23), he coveted the spoil of his people, and they surrendered it to him (v. 24).

Gideon's indulgence in sex and his greediness for gold led to idolatry. Greediness is idolatry (Col. 3:5), and both fornication and greediness are linked to idol worship (Eph. 5:5). Even King Solomon, who began as a God-fearing and God-loving person, eventually became an idol worshipper through his many foreign wives (1 Kings 11:4). Gideon made an ephod with the gold he had taken from the people, and this ephod became an idol to the children of Israel (Judg. 8:27). As a result, Gideon's family and the entire society of Israel were corrupted. Gideon began by tearing down the altar of Baal and its idol, but after his success he built something idolatrous. This failure canceled all his success.

Judges is a book concerning the enjoyment of the good land, which is a type of Christ. Gideon's success indicates the gaining of an excellent opportunity to enjoy Christ, but his failure indicates the losing of the opportunity to enjoy Christ. His failure shows us that we need to exercise strict control in dealing with the matters of sex and wealth. Otherwise, we will suffer the loss of the enjoyment of Christ. Any indulgence in these things will cause our enjoyment of Christ to be annulled.

Let us now go on to consider the many details of the fourth cycle of Israel's miserable history recorded in 6:1—8:32.

IV. THE FOURTH CYCLE

A. Israel Again Doing
That Which Was Evil in the Sight of Jehovah

Once again the children of Israel did that which was evil in the sight of Jehovah (6:1a).

B. Jehovah Delivering Israel
into the Hand of Midian for Seven Years

Jehovah delivered Israel into the hand of Midian for seven years (vv. 1b-6a). The children of Israel made for themselves dens, caves, and strongholds in the mountains (v. 2). Whenever Israel sowed, Midian rose up with Amalek and the children of the east against Israel and came with their cattle and their tents like swarming locusts to destroy the produce of the land (vv. 3-5). Thus, "Israel was greatly impoverished because of Midian" (v. 6a).

C. The Children of Israel
Crying Out to Jehovah because of Midian

The children of Israel cried out to Jehovah because of Midian (vv. 6b-7).

D. Jehovah Sending a Prophet
to Reprove the Children of Israel

Jehovah sent a man who was a prophet to reprove the children of Israel (v. 8a).

1. Reminding Them
of Jehovah's Delivering Them from Egypt
and His Giving to Them the Land of Canaan

Through this prophet Jehovah reminded the children of Israel of His delivering them from the hand of the Egyptians and out of the hand of all who oppressed them. He also reminded them that He had driven out the Canaanites before them and had given to them the land of Canaan (vv. 8b-9).

2. Charging Them Not to Fear
the Gods of the Amorites

Jehovah charged the children of Israel not to fear the gods of the Amorites, but they did not listen to His voice (v. 10).

E. The Angel of Jehovah (Christ)
Calling Gideon

In verses 11 through 24 we have an account of the Angel of Jehovah (Christ) calling Gideon.

1. Appearing to Him

In verses 11 through 13 we are told that the Angel of Jehovah appeared to Gideon. The Angel of Jehovah came and sat under the terebinth that was in Ophrah while Gideon was beating out the wheat in the winepress in order to hide it from the Midianites. In this way the Angel of Jehovah appeared to Gideon and said to him, "Jehovah is with you, valiant warrior" (v. 12).

2. Charging Him to Save Israel
from the Hand of Midian

The Angel of Jehovah charged Gideon to save Israel from the hand of the Midianites (vv. 14-16). He turned to Gideon and said, "Go in this strength of yours, and save Israel from the hand of Midian. Have I not sent you?" (v. 14). When Gideon asked by what way he could save Israel, the Angel of Jehovah said to him, "Surely I will be with you, and you will strike the Midianites as one man" (v. 16).

3. Performing a Sign for Him
by Receiving His Offering

Gideon asked the Angel of Jehovah to perform a sign for him that it was He who was speaking with him (vv. 17-24). The Angel of Jehovah performed a sign by receiving Gideon's offering. "The Angel of Jehovah put forth the end of the staff that was in His hand and touched the flesh and the unleavened cakes. And fire came up from the rock and consumed the flesh and the unleavened cakes. And the Angel of Jehovah went from his sight" (v. 21). This sign resulted in Gideon's building up of an altar to Jehovah, calling it Jehovah-shalom, which means "Jehovah is peace" or "Jehovah of peace" (v. 24).

F. Jehovah Charging Gideon
to Tear Down the Altar of Baal
That Belonged to His Father

Jehovah charged Gideon to tear down the altar of Baal that belonged to his father and to cut down the Asherah that was beside it and then to build an altar to Jehovah his God upon the top of that stronghold in the ordered manner (vv. 25-32).

1. Gideon Doing It by Ten Men at Night

Gideon did this by ten men at night and not by day because he was too afraid of his father's house and the men of the city (v. 27).

2. The Men of the City Contending for Baal

The men of the city contended for Baal (vv. 28-31). When they saw that the altar of Baal had been torn down and that the Asherah beside it had been cut down, they asked who had done this thing. After inquiring and seeking about, they concluded that Gideon had done it, and they desired to kill him.

3. Gideon Being Called Jerubbaal because of This

Because of this Gideon was called Jerubbaal, which means "Let Baal contend" (v. 32).

G. All the Midianites, Amalekites, and the Children of the East Gathering Together to Encamp in the Valley of Jezreel, and the Spirit of Jehovah Clothing Gideon

All the Midianites, Amalekites, and the children of the east gathered together, and they crossed over and encamped in the valley of Jezreel (v. 33). The Spirit of Jehovah clothed Gideon, and he blew his trumpet to call the Abiezrites. Then he sent messengers to call the people of Manasseh, Asher, Zebulun, and Naphtali to come up to meet them (vv. 34-35).

H. Gideon Asking God for Signs to Water a Fleece of Wool and to Dry It

According to verses 36 through 40, Gideon asked God for signs to water a fleece of wool and to dry it. First, Gideon said that if there was dew on the fleece alone and it was dry on the ground, then he would know that Jehovah would save Israel through his hand. The next morning there was dew only on the fleece. Then Gideon asked that it be dry on the fleece only and that there be dew on all the ground. God did so that night, and it was dry on the fleece only.

I. The Three Hundred Chosen by God to Follow Gideon to Defeat Midian for Israel

In 7:2-8a we see that three hundred were chosen by God to follow Gideon to defeat Midian for Israel. Jehovah told

Gideon that the people who were with him were too many for Jehovah to deliver Midian into their hand. God charged Gideon to proclaim that whoever was afraid and trembling should return and depart. Twenty-two thousand of the people returned, and ten thousand remained (vv. 2-3). Out of the ten thousand, only three hundred who lapped the water into their mouth with their hand were chosen by Jehovah (vv. 4-8a).

J. The Defeat of Midian

Judges 7:8b-25 describes the defeat of Midian.

1. By Gideon Hearing the Account of a Dream in the Camp of Midian

According to verses 9 through 15, Gideon heard the account of a dream in the camp of Midian. One of the Midianites recounted a dream to his companion, saying, "I have just had a dream. There was this round loaf of barley bread tumbling through the camp of Midian. And it came to the tent and struck it, so that it fell and turned upside down. And the tent collapsed" (v. 13). His companion responded by saying that this was nothing else than the sword of Gideon and that God had delivered Midian and all the camp into Gideon's hand. When Gideon heard the account of the dream and its interpretation, he worshipped, returned to the camp of Israel, and said, "Arise, for Jehovah has delivered the camp of Midian into your hand" (v. 15).

2. By the Three Hundred Men of Gideon Divided into Three Companies Blowing the Trumpets and Shattering the Pitchers

Gideon divided the three hundred men into three companies and put trumpets into their hands, as well as empty pitchers, with torches inside the pitchers (v. 16). They blew the trumpets and shattered the pitchers. Then, holding the torches in their left hands and the trumpets in their right hands, they cried out, "A sword for Jehovah and for Gideon!" (vv. 19-20). Then the whole camp of the Midianites ran off, and they shouted and fled.

3. By Jehovah Setting
Each Man's Sword against His Companion

Jehovah set each man's sword against his companion and against the whole camp (v. 22).

4. By the Men of Israel
Pursuing after the Midianites

The men of Israel from Naphtali, Asher, Manasseh, and Ephraim pursued after the Midianites (vv. 23-24).

5. The Two Princes of Midian Being Slain

The children of Israel captured two princes of Midian, Oreb and Zeeb, and slew them (v. 25).

K. The Complaint of Ephraim
and Gideon's Pacification

The men of Ephraim contended sharply with Gideon, complaining that he did not call them when he went to battle against Midian (8:1). Gideon pacified them by asking what he had done to compare with them and saying that it was into their hand that God gave the princes of Midian. Then their hostile spirit toward him subsided (vv. 2-3).

L. The Despising and Insulting
of the Men of Succoth and Penuel
toward Gideon

In verses 4 through 9 and 13 through 17 we see the despising and insulting of the men of Succoth and Penuel toward Gideon and the punishment of the men of Succoth and Penuel by Gideon.

M. Gideon Further Pursuing
the Midian Camps

After slaying one hundred twenty thousand men, Gideon further pursued the Midian camps of fifteen thousand men and captured and slew the two kings of Midian (vv. 10-12, 18-21).

N. Gideon's Dealing with the Men of Israel

Verses 22 through 28 speak concerning Gideon's dealing with the men of Israel.

1. Not Willing to Rule over Them

The men of Israel asked Gideon to rule over them, but he refused, saying, "I will not rule over you, nor will my son rule over you. Jehovah will rule over you" (vv. 22-23).

2. Asking Them for Their Spoils of Gold and Purple Garments

Gideon asked that each of them give him an earring of gold from his spoil, and they willingly did so, giving him one thousand seven hundred shekels of gold, in addition to crescents, pendants, and purple garments (vv. 24-26).

3. Making an Ephod with Gold and Placing It in His City

Gideon made an ephod with the gold and placed it in his city, in Ophrah. All Israel went as harlots to the ephod there, and it became a snare to Gideon and his house (v. 27).

4. Midian Being Subdued by Israel, and the Land of Israel Having Rest Forty Years

Midian was subdued before the children of Israel, and the land of Israel had rest forty years in the days of Gideon (v. 28).

O. Gideon's Family and His Decease

Chapter eight concludes with a word regarding Gideon's family and his decease (vv. 29-32).

1. Gideon Having Seventy Sons by Many Wives

Gideon had seventy sons by many wives. He also had another son, by the name of Abimelech, by his concubine in Shechem (vv. 30-31).

2. Gideon Dying at a Good Age

Gideon died at a good age, and he was buried in the tomb of his father in Ophrah (v. 32).

LIFE-STUDY OF JUDGES

THE MISERABLE HISTORY
OF ISRAEL'S FORSAKING OF GOD
CHAPTERS 2—16

(4)

THE FIFTH CYCLE
OF ISRAEL'S MISERABLE HISTORY

Scripture Reading: Judg. 8:33—10:5

The intrinsic significance of the fifth and sixth cycles of Israel's miserable history (8:33—10:5; 10:6—12:15) consists of Israel's forsaking God and joining herself to idols. This means that Israel divorced God, her legitimate Husband, and went after many idols.

Man's forsaking of God began in Genesis 3. God created man with a spirit so that man could contact Him, receive Him, and take Him in as life. The tree of life in the garden signified God Himself as the embodiment of life for us to contact and receive. God warned man not to partake of the other tree, the tree of the knowledge of good and evil, for eating of the fruit of that tree would issue in death. However, from the beginning of man's existence, Satan has been seducing man to take of the tree of the knowledge of good and evil, which is the embodiment of Satan himself. To take the tree of knowledge is actually to marry Satan and divorce God.

This forsaking of God and joining to Satan is the strongest factor behind the chaos in human society. Due to man's forsaking of God and joining to Satan, the entire world, including every nation, society, and family, has become chaotic. Immediately after man forsook God and joined himself to Satan, chaos came in. The first manifestation of this chaos was the first murder, which took place in Adam's family when Cain slew Abel. From that time onward, there has been chaos in every nation, society, and family. Gideon's failure was due to his forsaking of God and his joining himself to Satan. In his success he was joined to God, but in his failure he joined himself to Satan. When he joined himself to Satan, the issue was murder. He also indulged in the flesh, coveted, and committed idolatry. This issued in the corruption of his family and the entire society of Israel.

Even religion is part of the universal chaos. The world spoken of in Galatians 6:14 is not the secular world but the religious world. Christ died to save us from the religious world (1:4). In man's eyes religion is good, but in God's eyes every kind of religion is a section of the satanic world. In principle, the situation in today's Christianity is the same as the universal situation of the human race—it has forsaken God and joined itself to Satan.

We have also had periods of chaos in the Lord's recovery. It seems that in the recovery there are cycles of rebellion about every ten years, involving struggles for power to fulfill ambitions. The recent rebellion among us had two roots—unforgiven offenses and unfulfilled ambitions. The intrinsic significance of all these rebellions is forsaking God to go along with Satan. Satan fell because of ambition. To go along with Satan is to enter into the ambition that was present in Satan when he fell. He wanted to ascend to the throne; he wanted to be like the Most High (Isa. 14:13-14). Hence, to forsake God and join with Satan is to enter into the intrinsic ambition within this evil one.

The result of rebellion has always been chaos, with the rebellious ones causing damage to themselves. The churches that joined the recent rebellion have become barren and have even decreased in number, while the remaining churches have increased.

In family life, whenever a husband and a wife love the Lord and reject everything other than Him, their married life will be wonderful. But once a husband or wife begins to love something else in place of the Lord, their married life and family life become chaotic.

We have no right to divorce the Lord; we have no basis to forsake Him. We must take Him, love Him, honor Him, respect Him, regard Him, exalt Him, and cling to Him, rejecting Satan to the uttermost. Then we will be blessed.

This principle can be applied to the entire human race, to every nation, to every society, to every family, and to every individual. If we love the Lord and hate Satan, we will be blessed. However, we will only get into trouble whenever we change and begin to love something other than Christ. Psalm 33:12 says, "Blessed is the nation whose God is Jehovah." Blessed is everyone—nation, society, group, and individual— whose Lord, Head, King, and Husband is Jehovah.

At this point, let us turn to Judges 8:33—10:5, which covers yet another cycle of Israel's miserable history.

I. THE FIFTH CYCLE

A. Israel Turning Again and Going as Harlots after the Baalim

As soon as Gideon died, Israel turned again and went as harlots after the Baalim, making Baal-berith their god. They did not remember Jehovah their God, who had delivered them from the hand of all their enemies all around, nor did they show mercy to the house of Gideon for all the good he had done to Israel (8:33-35).

B. Abimelech, the Son of Jerubbaal, Gideon, Slaying His Brothers

Abimelech, the son of Jerubbaal, Gideon, slew his brothers, the sons of Jerubbaal, seventy men, on one stone (9:1-5). He was supported by his mother's brothers, all the family of his mother's father, and all the men of Shechem (vv. 1-3). They supported Abimelech with seventy pieces of silver from the temple of the idol Baal-berith, with which he hired worthless and wanton men to follow him (v. 4). However, the youngest son of Jerubbaal, Jotham, was left, for he hid himself (v. 5).

C. The Men of Shechem and All the House of Millo Making Abimelech King at Shechem

The men of Shechem and all the house of Millo made Abimelech king at Shechem (v. 6).

D. Jotham Protesting against Abimelech

Jotham protested against Abimelech (vv. 7-21). He likened Abimelech not to a good olive tree or a good fig tree or a good vine but, derisively, to an evil bramble (vv. 7-15). Then he cursed the men of Shechem, the house of Millo, and Abimelech with God's punishment over them (vv. 16-20). After Jotham did this, he ran off and fled (v. 21).

E. Abimelech Ruling over Israel Three Years

Abimelech ruled over Israel three years (v. 22).

F. God Sending an Evil Spirit between Abimelech and the Men of Shechem for the Punishment over Abimelech and the Men of Shechem

God sent an evil spirit between Abimelech and the men of Shechem, and they dealt treacherously with him, so that the violence done to the seventy sons of Jerubbaal might be avenged and so that their blood might be upon Abimelech their brother and upon the men of Shechem, who strengthened him to slay his brothers (vv. 23-24).

G. The Men of Shechem Dealing Treacherously with Abimelech

The men of Shechem dealt treacherously with Abimelech, revolting against him and being strengthened by Gaal the son of Ebed (vv. 25-29).

H. Zebul the Ruler of the City Helping Abimelech to Defeat Gaal and the Men of Shechem

Zebul the ruler of the city helped Abimelech to defeat Gaal and the men of Shechem, tear down the city of Shechem, and set its stronghold on fire to burn about a thousand men and women who escaped there (vv. 30-49).

I. God Repaying the Evil of Abimelech and All the Evil of the Men of Shechem

Abimelech went to take Thebez. When he came up to the tower and fought against it, a certain woman threw a millstone upon Abimelech's head, and it cracked his skull. He immediately called to the young man who bore his armor and told him to draw his sword and kill him, lest people say that he was slain by a woman. The young man pierced him through, and he died. Thus, God repaid the evil of Abimelech and all the evil of the men of Shechem, and the curse of Jotham came upon them (vv. 50-57).

After considering chapter nine of Judges, we can see that it presents to us a picture of what a mess God's elect Israel had become and to what extent they had degraded. Their degradation was initiated in their forsaking of Jehovah their God and their worshipping of the idols of the Canaanites, which issued in their indulgence in fleshly lust by having many wives to produce many sons. Gideon produced seventy-two sons of many wives (8:30-31; 9:5); another judge produced thirty sons (10:4); another judge produced thirty sons and thirty daughters (12:8-9); and another judge produced forty sons and thirty grandsons (vv. 13-14). Israel's degradation also issued in the wantonness of their hatred in slaying one another, ending themselves in full destruction.

J. Tola Rising Up to Save Israel

After Abimelech, Tola, a man of Issachar, rose up to save Israel, and he judged Israel twenty-three years. After Tola, Jair the Gileadite, who had thirty sons, rose up and judged Israel twenty-two years (10:1-5).

LIFE-STUDY OF JUDGES

THE MISERABLE HISTORY
OF ISRAEL'S FORSAKING OF GOD
CHAPTERS 2—16

(5)

THE SIXTH CYCLE
OF ISRAEL'S MISERABLE HISTORY

Scripture Reading: Judg. 10:6—12:15

I have the burden to speak further concerning forsaking God and being joined to Satan. This matter is fully revealed and recorded in the Scriptures. The first man was poisoned by this, and the first family was devastated by this. Ever since the time of Genesis 3, man has been forsaking God and joining to Satan, taking many things as replacements of God. In his fourteen Epistles, Paul ministered the all-inclusive and all-extensive Christ, but he also dealt with all kinds of replacements of Christ.

The book of Judges shows us how degraded and corrupt Israel had become. It is hard to imagine that the children of Israel, who had been chosen, taught, trained, and disciplined by God and who had God's law, could have become so rotten. Their degradation began with their forsaking of God and their worshipping of idols, and it issued in their indulgence in fleshly lust and in wanton self-destruction. Samson, the last judge mentioned in this book, was very powerful, yet the factor of his failure was his indulgence in sex. At the end of Judges, there is an account of wanton slaughter, describing how the entire tribe of Benjamin was nearly extinguished by Israel. The factor that led to this degradation was that they forsook God to the uttermost and turned to idols. Here we see that idol worship is closely linked to fornication and murder. If someone becomes an idol worshipper, he will become a person who is very indulgent in sex and full of hatred toward others.

I have been serving the Lord for nearly sixty-one years and have had much consideration concerning these matters. My realization is that all the sins, all the evils, all the iniquities, come out of one source—forsaking God and joining to something which becomes a replacement of God. This is true even in small things. For example, a sister's combing of her hair can be an idol. If a sister pays too much attention to her hair, honoring it excessively, that kind of honor is a worship. Such a sister may not have time in the morning to spend ten minutes with the Lord, but she has plenty of time to comb her hair. The sisters may need to check with the Lord regarding this, saying, "Lord, is the way I care for my hair a replacement of You?" If a sister checks with the Lord in this way, the Lord will tell her, her conscience will tell her, and her intuition in her spirit will also tell her.

In recent years, certain ones left us and formed divisions. It seems that the leaders among them are doing nothing but traveling from place to place in order to create and strengthen such divisions. Division has become a thing that motivates and energizes them. The goal of their activity is to separate the saints from the enjoyment of the New Testament ministry. Their intention is to poison the saints in order to deaden them, cool them down, and cause them to have doubts about the Lord's recovery. The main factor with these ones is that they have left the church and joined themselves to the "demon" of division.

I have published a book called *The Fermentation of the Present Rebellion*, presenting the whole story, fully documented. That book concludes by saying that we need to "reject any kind of division (1 Cor. 1:10), to stand against any wind of teaching and any spreading of spiritual death (Eph. 4:14; 2 Tim. 2:16-17), and to separate ourselves from the contagious ones—exercising to quarantine" (Titus 3:10; Rom. 16:17). Some, however, have not agreed to quarantine these ones and have embraced division. They have been deceived to such an extent that they take the matter of division as an idol.

In our spiritual life, even to take a small thing, such as combing our hair or buying something, may be to take another husband. To some extent, this is to forsake Christ. Even in holding a thought preferring this or that thing, our preference can become an idol. You may say that you are still with the Lord, but you may be with the Lord in a general way, but particularly, in a certain thing, you may not be with the Lord.

God's Spirit is indwelling us and is speaking to us all the time. Sometimes I would like to speak something to my wife, even something spiritual, but someone within is saying, "Don't talk." To take my preference to speak that thing would be to make that thing an idol and would bring me into chaos. But to obey the inner speaking is to hold to our one Lord, one Master, one Head, one Husband.

Let us now turn to Judges 10:6—12:15 and consider the sixth cycle of Israel's miserable history.

<h3 style="text-align:center">VI. THE SIXTH CYCLE</h3>

A. Israel Again Doing That Which Was Evil in the Sight of Jehovah

Israel again did that which was evil in the sight of Jehovah. They served the Baalim, the Ashtaroth, the gods of Aram, the gods of Sidon, the gods of Moab, the gods of the Ammonites, and the gods of the Philistines, forsaking Jehovah and not serving Him (10:6).

B. The Anger of Jehovah Burning against Israel

The anger of Jehovah burned against Israel, and Jehovah sold them into the hand of the Philistines and of the Amorites, who oppressed them eighteen years. The children of Israel were greatly distressed (vv. 7-9).

C. Israel Crying Out to Jehovah

The children of Israel cried out to Jehovah, saying, "We have sinned against You, for we have forsaken our God and have served the Baalim" (v. 10). Then they prayed for deliverance and returned to Jehovah (vv. 15-16a).

D. Jehovah's Rebuking of Israel

In verses 11 through 14 we have Jehovah's rebuking of Israel. First, He asked them if He had not saved them from the Egyptians, the Amorites, the children of Ammon, and the Philistines. He also reminded them that He saved them when they were oppressed by the Sidonians, Amalek, and Maon. Then He went on to say, "But you forsook Me and served other gods; therefore I will not save you again. Go and cry out to the gods that you have chosen. Let them save you in the time of your distress" (vv. 13-14).

E. Jehovah Being Unable to Bear Israel's Misery

In verse 16b we are told that Jehovah was no longer able to bear Israel's misery.

F. The Pressure of the Ammonites and the Need of a Head over Israel to Take the Lead to Fight against the Ammonites

Verses 17 and 18 speak of the pressure of the Ammonites and the need of a head over Israel to take the lead to fight against the Ammonites. The princes of Gilead said each to his companion, "Who is the man who will begin to fight against the children of Ammon? He shall be head over all the inhabitants of Gilead" (v. 18).

G. The Rising Up of Jephthah

Judges 11:1-11 records the rising up of Jephthah, a mighty man of Gilead, the son of a harlot. He was rejected by his stepbrothers but was received by the worthless men (vv. 2-3). Eventually, he was requested by the elders of Gilead to be their head and chief to fight the Ammonites for them (vv. 4-11).

H. Jephthah's Negotiation with the King of the Ammonites

Jephthah negotiated with the king of the Ammonites. His negotiation was based upon the fact that during a history of three hundred years, there had been no reason for the

Ammonites to fight against Israel (vv. 12-27). However, the king of the Ammonites did not listen to the words of Jephthah (v. 28).

I. Jehovah's Spirit Coming upon Jephthah, and Jehovah Delivering the Ammonites into His Hand

The Spirit of Jehovah came upon Jephthah, and Jehovah delivered the Ammonites into His hand (vv. 29-32).

J. Jephthah Defeating the Ammonites

Jephthah defeated the Ammonites and took their twenty cities. Thus the Ammonites were subdued before the children of Israel (v. 33).

K. Jephthah Making a Vow to Jehovah

In verses 30 and 31 Jephthah made a vow to Jehovah. According to verses 34 through 40, Jephthah's daughter kept this vow with her whole life's virginity.

L. The Ephraimites Quarreling with Jephthah, and Jephthah Fighting against Them

In 12:1-6 we see that the Ephraimites quarreled with Jephthah and that he fought against them.

M. Jephthah Judging Israel Six Years

Jephthah judged Israel six years. Then he died and was buried in one of the cities of Gilead. After him, Ibzan, who had thirty sons and thirty daughters, judged Israel seven years (vv. 7-9). Ibzan died and was buried in Bethlehem, and then Elon the Zebulunite judged Israel ten years. He was followed by Abdon the Pirathonite, who had forty sons and thirty grandsons, judging Israel eight years. In total, these judges judged Israel thirty-one years (vv. 10-15).

THE MISERABLE HISTORY
OF ISRAEL'S FORSAKING OF GOD
CHAPTERS 2—16

(6)

THE SEVENTH CYCLE
OF ISRAEL'S MISERABLE HISTORY

Scripture Reading: Judg. 13:1—16:31

The book of Judges records seven cycles of Israel's miserable history of forsaking God. In reading through these cycles in Judges, it is difficult to understand how someone as positive as Gideon could become so negative. Between his success and his failure, it must have been that a demon entered him, because he forsook God and joined himself to Satan.

This principle can be seen even more in the case of Samson. His birth was a miracle initiated by the appearing of the Angel of Jehovah. When Samson was in the bosom of his mother, he was sanctified to be a Nazarite. As he grew up, he was clean and pure according to God's ordination, and he was empowered by the Spirit of God. When the Israelites were under the tyranny of the Philistines, the Spirit of God as the holy, economical Spirit came upon Samson, and he became powerful.

However, Samson's unique problem was in the matter of sex. He was not genuine in seeking for a spouse; rather, his contacting of women was just to indulge his lusts. He indulged his lust with a Philistine woman, with a harlot in Gaza, and with a woman named Delilah. Although he had been empowered by God, he was damaged and destroyed to the uttermost because of his indulgence in lust.

Shortly after I decided to give up my job and serve the Lord, I went to Shanghai to see Brother Nee. He told me that in serving the Lord the brothers must learn the principle of not contacting a female, especially a young one, in private. I was deeply impressed by this, and from that time I have practiced Brother Nee's instructions and have also passed them on to the saints.

The sisters should clothe and cover their body in a proper way. First Timothy 2:9 charges the sisters to "adorn themselves in proper clothing with modesty and sobriety, not with braided hair and gold or pearls or costly clothing." The word *proper* denotes fitting to the sisters' nature and position as saints of God. In Greek the word for *clothing* implies deportment, demeanor. A sister's demeanor, of which clothing is the main sign, must befit her saintly position. The word *modesty* means, literally, "shamefastness," denoting being bound or made fast by an honorable shame (Vincent), implying not forward or overbold but moderate, observing the proprieties of womanhood. The word *sobriety* means "sobermindedness, self-restraint; the restricting of oneself soberly and discreetly." The sisters in a local church should clothe themselves with these two virtues—shamefastness and self-restraint—as their demeanor.

Hebrews 13:4 says, "Let marriage be held in honor among all," because through marriage mankind continues to exist on earth and is propagated to replenish the earth. God created a need and desire within man to be married. A desire to be married is not sinful; on the contrary, it is according to God's ordination. However, the time to consider marriage is after graduation from college. All the brothers and sisters should consecrate to the Lord, giving themselves to Him and promising that they will live for Him and even live Him their entire life. Then they should pray to see if there is the leading of the Lord in this matter, rather than trying to be too selective. Keeping these items will be a great protection to the young people.

At this juncture, let us consider the details concerning Samson recorded in Judges 13:1—16:31.

VII. THE SEVENTH CYCLE

A. Israel Again Doing That Which Was Evil in the Sight of Jehovah

The children of Israel again did that which was evil in the sight of Jehovah (13:1a).

B. Jehovah Delivering Israel into the Hand of the Philistines Forty Years

Jehovah delivered the children of Israel into the hand of the Philistines forty years (v. 1b).

C. The Performance of Samson

1. His Origin

In verses 3 through 23 we have an account of Samson's origin.

a. His Father Manoah Being of the Family of the Danites, and His Mother Being Barren

Samson's father, Manoah, was of the family of the Danites. His wife was barren and had borne no children (v. 2).

b. His Conception

1) A Miracle Initiated by the Appearing of the Angel of Jehovah (Christ)

Samson's conception was actually a miracle initiated by the appearing of the Angel of Jehovah (Christ) to his mother and father. Verse 3 says, "The Angel of Jehovah appeared to the woman and said to her, Now you are barren and have borne no children; but you will conceive and bear a son." When she told her husband about this, he entreated Jehovah, saying, "Oh, Lord! Let the man of God, whom You sent, come again to us, I pray; and let Him teach us what we should do with the child that is to be born" (v. 8). God hearkened to the voice of Manoah, and the Angel of God came again to the woman. She went to tell her husband, and he followed her. When Manoah asked the Angel of Jehovah what His name was, He said, "Why do you ask about My name, since it is wonderful?" (v. 18).

2) To Be a Nazarite Boy

Samson was to be a Nazarite boy, who was not to drink wine, nor to eat anything unclean, nor to cut his hair with a razor, so that he would save Israel from the hand of the Philistines (vv. 3-5, 7).

2. His Birth and Growth

a. Born to Be Called Samson

Verse 24a says that the woman bore a son and called his name Samson. The name *Samson* means "sunlike."

b. Growing as a Nazarite by the Blessing of Jehovah

Samson grew as a Nazarite by the blessing of Jehovah (v. 24b).

1) With the Head Covered

Samson grew up with his head covered. This was signified by his not cutting his hair (v. 5).

2) In the Submission to God

Samson was in submission to God. This was signified by the keeping of his long hair (cf. 1 Cor. 11:15).

3) Without Touching Worldly Pleasures

As a Nazarite, Samson grew up without touching worldly pleasures. This was signified by his not drinking wine (Judg. 13:7a).

4) In Keeping Himself Clean

Samson also kept himself clean. This was signified by his not eating the unclean things (v. 7b).

3. Moved by the Spirit of God

Samson was moved by the Spirit of God (v. 25).

4. His Faith in God

Samson had faith in God (cf. Heb. 11:32). His faith is seen in his tearing a young lion by the Spirit of Jehovah rushing upon him (14:5-6), in his slaying thirty men by the Spirit of Jehovah rushing upon him (v. 19), and in his destroying the house where he was compelled to perform (16:28-30).

5. His Might

Chapters fourteen through sixteen describe a number of instances of Samson's might. We see his might in his tearing a young lion by the Spirit of Jehovah and in his killing thirty men by the Spirit rushing upon him (14:5-6, 19). We see his might in his catching three hundred foxes (15:4). According to verses 12 through 16, Samson's might was displayed in his breaking the two ropes with which he was bound and in his killing one thousand men by the Spirit of Jehovah rushing upon him. Moreover, Samson's might was shown in his plucking up the doors of the gate of the city and the two posts with the bar and bringing them up to the top of the mountain in front of Hebron (16:3). The last case of Samson's might was in his destroying the house where he performed (vv. 29-30).

6. His Failure

Samson failed in not contacting God and in indulging in sex. He indulged in sex with a woman of the Philistines, whom he married and who released his secret to the Philistines (14:1-3, 10-17); with a harlot in Gaza, in whose place Samson was surrounded by the Philistines (16:1-3); and with a woman by the name of Delilah, who released the secret of his great strength (vv. 4-20a).

7. His Miserable Ending

Judges 16:20b-30 is a record of Samson's miserable ending. First, Jehovah left him (v. 20b). Then the Philistines grabbed him, gouged out his eyes, and bound him with fetters, and he ground at the mill in the prison house (v. 21). He was forced to perform before the Philistines that they might celebrate their victory over him before their god Dagon (vv. 23-25). Finally, Samson was killed by the house which was destroyed by him (vv. 28-30).

8. Samson Judging Israel Twenty Years

The record in Judges regarding Samson concludes with the word saying that he had judged Israel twenty years (v. 31b).

LIFE-STUDY OF JUDGES

MESSAGE NINE

THE STINKING STORY
OF ISRAEL'S CORRUPTION BEFORE GOD
CHAPTERS 17—21

(1)

THE ABOMINABLE CHAOS IN THEIR WORSHIP

Scripture Reading: Judg. 17—18

In this life-study of the books of Joshua, Judges, and Ruth, we are concerned not with history but with learning from the types how to gain Christ and enjoy Him. The history contained in these books is a great type that shows how God's elect can gain and enjoy the good land, which is a complete and all-inclusive type of Christ. Even the small details show us the secret of gaining and enjoying Christ, just as in our daily life something as small as shopping for an article of clothing can be a factor in whether or not we obtain Christ and enjoy Christ.

When we were saved, we were brought into a fellowship of the Divine Trinity with His redeemed and regenerated people. From that time God and we have been in a fellowship. First John 1:3 says, "That which we have seen and heard we report also to you that you also may have fellowship with us, and indeed our fellowship is with the Father and with His Son Jesus Christ." This fellowship is between the apostles and God and between the believers and the apostles. The full salvation of God is in this fellowship. It is in this fellowship that we can gain what God has given us, that is, the Son of God given to us by God as our allotted portion.

If we remain in this fellowship, we will have the way to gain and enjoy Christ. If our fellowship with God is cut off, we will lose our enjoyment immediately. Concerning this, the

Lord Jesus uses the word *abide* and speaks of our abiding in Him as the vine (John 15:4). The vine is a figure of the all-inclusive Christ under God's cultivation. As long as the branch abides in the vine, there is fellowship. But once a branch ceases to abide in the vine, the branch is cut off, becomes barren and dry, and loses the enjoyment of the riches of the vine (vv. 5-6).

The fellowship of life is not a rough matter but is very fine. Even a little word spoken with an improper attitude is enough to cut us off from the fellowship of life.

Our enjoyment of Christ is essential. Our fellowship can speed up the turning of the great wheel of God's move in the universe. But if we are cut off from the fellowship just a little, God's economy will not be able to go forward for a period of time. Therefore, we need to be careful every day and in every detail, keeping ourselves in the enjoyment of Christ all the time. Then God's economy will be able to go forward.

In Revelation 22:20 the Lord Jesus said, "I come quickly," but today there is no sign that He is coming, because the wheel has not had an adequate opportunity to turn. If the saints in the Lord's recovery take care of all the items of the intrinsic significances of the books of Joshua, Judges, and Ruth, the Lord will be able to come back much sooner. However, doing things without taking care of the inner feeling, the sense of life within, may delay the Lord for a long time.

The rebellion that took place in 1959-1965 in Taiwan delayed the Lord very much. When we began the ministry there in 1949, we increased nearly a hundred-fold in just a few years. Since the rebellion the rate of increase has never been the same. The recent rebellion in the recovery has also delayed the Lord and, in certain respects, hindered the move of the wheel of God's economy. For this reason, I have been stressing the intrinsic significances in Joshua and Judges. I have been doing this not only to show that God has given us Christ as the good land but also to show how we can possess and enjoy this land for generations to come.

Being saved is easy, but remaining in the fellowship with God to enjoy Christ is not easy. Many fundamental Christians preach that Christ, the Son of God, is the Savior of sinners, but they may know very little, if anything, about the fellowship with the Triune God.

At this juncture, let us consider the situation of Israel as it is presented in Judges 17 and 18. In their degradation Israel became chaotic in three ways: in government, in worship, and in morality. They had no government, no administration. God's tabernacle was at Shiloh, and the high priest had the Urim and Thummim, but there was no administration. Judges 17 and 18 reveal the abominable chaos in the children of Israel's worship. Micah set up a house of gods in his home. His mother consecrated silver to Jehovah to make an idol and a molten image. Micah then set up a house of gods, made an ephod and teraphim, and consecrated one of his sons to be his priest. The ephod signifies the authority of God, without which no one can worship God. Later, Micah consecrated a Levite to be his house priest, paying him a salary of ten pieces of silver a year plus an array of clothing and his food. In those days the Danites robbed Micah of his idol, the ephod, the teraphim, and the molten image with his priest, and with them they set up another worship place in the city of Dan, while God's tabernacle remained in Shiloh. The result was two worship centers—the proper one with God's tabernacle at Shiloh and the improper one in Dan. That was the chaos of the children of Israel in their worship.

We may apply this picture to the present situation of Christianity. Today's Christianity has many "houses of Micah," the most prominent of which is the Roman Catholic Church. The Roman Catholic Church has set up idols, made its own "ephod," and set up its own priests. According to the New Testament all those who are born of God should be priests (1 Pet. 2:5, 9), but Catholicism has hired its own priests and set up a hierarchy under a pope. In principle, Catholicism is the same as the house of Micah in Judges. The state churches, the denominations, and many of the independent groups are also houses of Micah, full of idols as replacements of Christ.

Not everything in Christianity is wrong, but everything is a mixture. It is like the woman who hid leaven in three measures of meal until the whole was leavened (Matt. 13:33). The meal signifies Christ as food for God and for His people. The leaven signifies evil things (1 Cor. 5:6, 8) and evil doctrines (Matt. 16:6, 11-12). Micah's mother offered something to God, but her offering to God was mixed with the leaven of idolatry. Today the same mixture and chaotic situation exists in Christianity.

Let us now turn to Judges 17 and 18 and consider what these chapters have to say regarding the abominable chaos in Israel's worship.

I. MICAH SETTING UP A HOUSE OF GODS IN HIS HOME

Judges 17:1-6 tells us that Micah, a man from the hill country of Ephraim, set up a house of gods in his house.

A. Taking Eleven Hundred Pieces of Silver from His Mother

Micah took eleven hundred pieces of silver from his mother without her knowing it (v. 2a).

B. Micah's Mother Uttering a Curse

Micah's mother uttered a curse and spoke it in his hearing (v. 2b).

C. Micah Confessing That He Stole the Silver

Micah confessed to his mother that he stole the silver, and she said, "Blessed of Jehovah be my son!" (v. 2c).

D. Micah Returning the Silver to His Mother

Micah returned the silver to his mother, and she consecrated the silver to Jehovah from her hand to her son to make an idol and a molten image. She gave two hundred pieces of the silver to the founder, who made them into an idol and a molten image (vv. 3-4).

E. Micah Setting Up a House of Gods and Making an Ephod and Teraphim and Consecrating One of His Sons to Become His Priest

Micah set up a house of gods. He also made an ephod and teraphim and consecrated one of his sons to become his priest (v. 5).

F. There Being No King in Israel, and Everyone Doing That Which Was Right in His Own Eyes

Verse 6 says that in those days there was no king in Israel; everyone did that which was right in his own eyes.

II. MICAH CONSECRATING A LEVITE TO BE HIS HOUSE PRIEST

In verses 7 through 13 we see that Micah consecrated a Levite to be his house priest.

A. The Levite Being a Young Man from Bethlehem in Judah

The Levite was a young man from Bethlehem in Judah, of the family of Judah. He was a sojourner, traveling in order to dwell wherever he could find a place (vv. 7-9).

B. Micah Asking This Young Man to Stay with Him

Micah asked this young man to stay with him and be a father and a priest to him, promising to pay him ten pieces of silver a year and an array of clothing and his food (v. 10).

C. The Levite Being Content to Stay with Micah Like One of His Sons

The Levite was content to stay with Micah, and the young man was to Micah like one of his sons (v. 11).

D. Micah Consecrating the Levite to Be His Priest in His House

Micah consecrated the Levite to be his priest in his house.

Then Micah said, "Now I know that Jehovah will prosper me, because the Levite has become my priest" (vv. 12-13).

III. THE DANITES ROBBING MICAH OF HIS SCULPTURED IDOL, THE EPHOD, THE TERAPHIM, AND THE MOLTEN IMAGE WITH HIS PRIEST

In chapter eighteen we see that the Danites robbed Micah of his sculptured idol, the ephod, the teraphim, and the molten image with his priest.

A. The Tribe of the Danites Seeking for Themselves an Inheritance to Dwell In

In those days there was no king in Israel, and the tribe of the Danites sought for themselves an inheritance to dwell in, for unto that day the lot had not fallen for them on an inheritance among the tribes of Israel (v. 1).

B. The Children of Dan Sending Five Men to Spy Out the Land and Search It Out

The children of Dan sent five men from among all of them, men of valor, to spy out the land and search it out. They came to the country of Ephraim, to the house of Micah, and they lodged there (v. 2).

C. The Five Men Asking the Levite to Inquire of God That They Might Know If Their Way Would Be Prosperous

The five men recognized the voice of the young Levite man, and they asked him, "Who brought you here? And what are you doing in this place? And what do you have here?" (v. 3). When the Levite explained that Micah had hired him to be his priest, they said to him, "Inquire now of God that we may know if our way on which we are going will be prosperous" (vv. 4-5).

D. The Priest Ordained by Micah Telling the Five Men to Go in Peace

The priest ordained by Micah said to the five men, "Go

in peace; your way on which you are going is before Jehovah"
(v. 6).

E. The Five Men Coming to Laish and Seeing the Life of the People

The five men left and came to Laish. They saw the people
who were in it, dwelling quiet and secure. Then they went
back to their brothers and asked them to go to take possession of the land, saying, "God has indeed delivered it into your
hand" (vv. 7-10).

F. Six Hundred Men Setting Out from the Family of Dan and Coming to the House of Micah

Six hundred men girded with weapons of war set out from
the family of Dan and came to the house of Micah in the hill
country of Ephraim (vv. 11-13).

G. The Five Men Who Had Gone to Spy the Land of Laish Speaking to the Levite concerning His Being a Priest for a Tribe and Family in Israel

The five men who had gone to spy the land of Laish
entered into the house of the young Levite, the house of
Micah, with six hundred men girded with weapons of war
standing at the entrance of the gate, to seize the sculptured
idol, the ephod, the teraphim, and the molten image. When
the priest asked them what they were doing, they said to him,
"Is it better for you to be a priest for the house of one man or a
priest for a tribe and family in Israel?" (vv. 14-19).

H. The Young Priest Taking the Ephod, the Teraphim, and the Sculptured Idol and Going into the Midst of the People

The young priest's heart was glad. He took the ephod, the
teraphim, and the sculptured idol and went into the midst of
the people. Thus, the Danites robbed Micah of all the idols
and the priest with which he worshipped God (vv. 20-26).

I. The Danites Coming to Laish
and Slaying the People

Taking the idols which Micah had made and the priest that had been his, the Danites came to Laish, slew the people, burned the city, and called the name of the city Dan, according to the name of Dan their father (vv. 27-29).

J. The Children of Dan
Erecting the Sculptured Idol

The children of Dan erected the sculptured idol. Jonathan the son of Gershom, the son of Moses, he and his sons, became priests to the tribe of Dan until the day of the captivity of the land. They set up the sculptured idol that Micah had made the whole time that the house of God was in Shiloh (vv. 30-31).

LIFE-STUDY OF JUDGES

MESSAGE TEN

THE STINKING STORY
OF ISRAEL'S CORRUPTION BEFORE GOD
CHAPTERS 17—21

(2)

THE SODOMITICAL CORRUPTION IN THEIR MORALITY
AND
THE TERRIBLE SLAUGHTER AMONG THEIR TRIBES

Scripture Reading: Judg. 19—21

Before we consider chapters nineteen through twenty-one, I would like to give a further word concerning the application of the account of Micah's house of idols (17:1-13) to the situation in Christianity today.

Any teaching or practice among Christians that is not according to the Scriptures is an idol. In the recent rebellion among us, a teaching regarding autonomy was promoted. Those who teach this stress that every local church is absolutely autonomous. However, this is contrary to the Scriptures and produces local sects. This teaching has become an idol.

In the United States every state is autonomous in business affairs, but the fifty states are not fifty different nations. On the contrary, there are fifty states but one nation. Likewise, each local church is autonomous in its business affairs, but the teaching that each local church is absolutely autonomous in every way within its locality is an idol. Nevertheless, some are using this teaching to spread division.

Every item in the Lord's recovery must be according to the Bible. For example, calling on the name of the Lord and pray-reading are scriptural practices (Gen. 4:26; 13:4; Eph. 6:17-18). When we call on the name of the Lord, our inner man is refreshed. When we pray-read the Word, we are fed.

The difference between the churches in the Lord's recovery and Christianity is that the local churches in the recovery try their best to do everything according to the Bible, the Word of God. The Bible reveals that the church as the Body of Christ is universally and uniquely one. Because all the members of the Body of Christ exist on earth in different cities, this unique Body of Christ is expressed among people on earth in many cities—one city, one church. Whereas Catholicism, the denominations, and the independent groups are "houses of Micah," we meet as a local church, as the church in a particular city. In the Scriptures there are no house churches, street churches, state churches, or district churches. Instead, there are local churches. The local church in a city is a part of the Body. Therefore, we practice the local churches, and we also practice the universal Body of Christ.

The intrinsic significance of the books of Joshua and Judges is that these books show us the detailed points of how to possess Christ, keep Christ, and enjoy Christ. We have seen that, according to the record in Judges, in the degradation Israel became chaotic in government, in worship, and in morality. Such a people surely could not gain Christ and enjoy Him. But we thank the Lord that, in the midst of the chaotic situation, there was a person—Boaz—who had the highest standard of morality. As we will see when we come to the book of Ruth, according to typology Boaz was one who enjoyed Christ very much.

Let us now look into what is recorded concerning Israel in the last three chapters of Judges.

I. THE SODOMITICAL CORRUPTION IN THEIR MORALITY

Chapter nineteen is a record of Israel's sodomitical corruption in their morality.

A. The Story of Corruption

Judges 19:1-26 tells a story of corruption. In those days, when there was no king in Israel, a certain Levite dwelling in the far end of the hill country of Ephraim took a concubine from Bethlehem in Judah (v. 1). The concubine went about as a harlot and departed from the Levite to her father's house, to Bethlehem in Judah, for four months (v. 2). Her husband rose up and came after her to speak to her affectionately and to bring her back (vv. 3-9). He brought her from her father's house, went through Jerusalem, and came to Gibeah, which belonged to Benjamin. He sat in the square of the city, but no one took them into his house to lodge them (vv. 10-15). In the evening an old man out of the field from his work saw the wayfarer in the square of the city and brought him and his concubine to his house and took them as his guests (vv. 16-21).

While they were making their hearts merry, the worthless men of the city surrounded the house, beating on the door. They spoke to the master of the house, saying, "Bring out the man who went into your house that we may know him" (v. 22). The old man, the master of the house, came out and said to them, "No, my brothers; do not do this evil thing, I beg you. Since this man has come into my house, do not commit this folly. Here is my virgin daughter and his concubine. Let me bring them out, I beg you; and humble them and do to them what seems good in your sight. But to this man do not do such folly" (vv. 23-24). But the worthless men did not want to listen to the old man; so the Levite took hold of his concubine and brought her out to them; and they knew her. They abused her all night long until morning (v. 25). In the early morning the concubine came and fell at the entrance of the old man's house, where her lord had been until it was light (v. 26).

B. The Spreading of This Story of Corruption throughout All the Territory of Israel

According to verses 27 through 30 the story of this corruption was spread throughout all the territory of Israel. The Levite rose up in the morning and opened the doors of the house and went out to go on his way. He discovered his concubine fallen at the entrance of the house with her hands upon the threshold (v. 27). He spoke to her, but there was no answer. He then put her upon the donkey and went to his place (v. 28). When he came to his house, he cut her up limb by limb into twelve pieces and sent her throughout all the territory of Israel (v. 29). When everyone saw this, they said, "No such thing has ever happened or been seen since the day the children of Israel went up out of the land of Egypt until this day. Consider it, and take counsel and speak" (v. 30).

II. THE TERRIBLE SLAUGHTER AMONG THEIR TRIBES

In chapters twenty and twenty-one we have an account of the terrible slaughter among their tribes.

A. All the Children of Israel Gathering as One Man unto Jehovah

All the children of Israel from Dan as far as Beer-sheba, with the land of Gilead, gathered as one man unto Jehovah. The leaders of all the people, of all the tribes of Israel, presented themselves in the congregation of the people of God at Mizpah, four hundred thousand footmen who drew the sword. The children of Benjamin heard about it (20:1-3a).

B. The Levite Telling Them the Story of the Wickedness and Folly of the Men of Gibeah

The Levite, the husband of the woman who had been murdered, told them the story of the wickedness and folly of the men of Gibeah. Then he asked all the children of Israel to give their advice and counsel (vv. 3b-7).

C. All the People Rising Up as One Man and, Knit Together as One Man, Being Gathered against the City of Gibeah

All the people rose up as one man, saying that none of them would go to their tents nor any of them return to their houses. Rather, they would go up against Gibeah by lot. Thus all the men of Israel, knit together as one man, were gathered against the city (vv. 8-11).

D. The Tribes of Israel Sending Men throughout the Tribe of Benjamin

The tribes of Israel sent men throughout the tribe of Benjamin, requesting them to deliver up the worthless men who were in Gibeah, for they would kill them and put away the evil from Israel (vv. 12-13a).

E. The Benjaminites Not Listening to the Voice of Their Brothers, the Children of Israel

The Benjaminites would not listen to the voice of their brothers, the children of Israel. The children of Benjamin gathered together at Gibeah from their cities to go to battle with the children of Israel, with twenty-six thousand men who drew the sword, apart from seven hundred choice men from Gibeah. These went out against four hundred thousand men of Israel who drew the sword, men of war (vv. 13b-17).

F. The Children of Israel Going Up to Bethel and Inquiring of God

The children of Israel went up to Bethel and inquired of God as to which of them should go up first into battle with the children of Benjamin, and Jehovah said, "Judah first" (v. 18).

G. The Children of Israel and the Children of Benjamin Coming into the Battle

The children of Israel and the children of Benjamin came into the battle, and on that day the children of Benjamin slew twenty-two thousand men of Israel (vv. 19-21).

H. The Children of Israel Going Up and Weeping before Jehovah, Inquiring of Him

The children of Israel went up and wept before Jehovah into the evening. They inquired of Jehovah, saying, "Shall I again approach the battle with the children of Benjamin my brother?" Jehovah said, "Go up against him" (vv. 22-23).

I. On the Second Day the Children of Israel Going to Fight with the Children of Benjamin

On the second day the children of Israel went to fight with the children of Benjamin, who slew another eighteen thousand men among the children of Israel (vv. 24-25).

J. All the Children of Israel
Going Up to Bethel and Weeping before Jehovah

All the children of Israel went up to Bethel and wept before Jehovah, fasting until the evening and offering burnt offerings and peace offerings before Jehovah. They inquired of Jehovah, saying, "Shall I again go out into battle with the children of Benjamin my brother, or shall I cease?" Jehovah answered, "Go up, for tomorrow I will deliver them into your hand" (vv. 26-28).

K. The Children of Israel Going Up
against the Children of Benjamin
on the Third Day

The children of Israel went up against the children of Benjamin on the third day and set themselves in array against Gibeah as at other times. First, the children of Benjamin slew about thirty men of Israel. Then the children of Israel destroyed twenty-five thousand one hundred men of Benjamin, by Jehovah striking them down before Israel (vv. 29-35).

L. The Ambush of Israel
Hurrying and Rushing against Gibeah and Slaying
the Whole City

The ambush of Israel hurried and rushed against Gibeah and slew the whole city (even though about thirty men were slain by the children of Benjamin) and burned the city. Then the children of Benjamin turned before the men of Israel toward the wilderness, but the children of Israel overtook them and killed twenty-five thousand of them on that day (vv. 36-46).

M. Six Hundred Men of the Children of Benjamin
Turning and Fleeing into the Wilderness

Six hundred men of the children of Benjamin turned and fled into the wilderness. The men of Israel returned to the children of Benjamin, striking them, both the entire city with

the cattle and all that was found there. Moreover, all the
cities that were found they set on fire (vv. 47-48).

N. The Children of Israel Being Grieved
concerning Benjamin Their Brother

The children of Israel were grieved concerning Benjamin
their brother that one tribe had been cut down from Israel
(21:1-6, 15).

O. The Children of Israel
Planning to Get Wives and Possessions
for the Remnant of Benjamin

In verses 7 through 24 we see that the children of Israel
planned to get wives and possessions for the remnant of
Benjamin. They sent twelve thousand of the valiant to destroy
the inhabitants of Jabesh-gilead. These captured four hundred young virgins to be wives of the Benjaminites (vv. 7-14).
In addition to this, the elders of the assembly commanded the
Benjaminites to catch the daughters of Shiloh to be their
wives, and the children of Benjamin did so (vv. 16-23a). Then
the Benjaminites went and dwelt in their inheritance and
they rebuilt the cities and dwelt in them (v. 23b).

P. In Those Days There Being No King in Israel,
and Each Man Doing
What Was Right in His Own Eyes

The book of Judges concludes by saying that in those days
there was no king in Israel; each man did what was right in
his own eyes (v. 25).

LIFE-STUDY OF RUTH

MESSAGE ONE

AN INTRODUCTORY WORD

Scripture Reading: Ruth 1:1-5; 2:1-2; 3:1; 4:9-10, 13, 21-22; Matt. 1:5-6

In this message we will give a brief introductory word to the Life-study of Ruth.

I. RUTH BEING AN APPENDIX
TO THE BOOK OF JUDGES, CONTEMPORARY WITH
THE FIRST HALF OF JUDGES

Ruth is an appendix to the book of Judges, contemporary with the first half of Judges. Judges is a book of Israel's miserable history, dark and stinking; Ruth is the record of a couple's excellent story, bright and aromatic. The main role in this story is like a lily growing out of brambles and a bright star in the dark night.

II. THE BOOK OF RUTH BEING
AN IMPORTANT PART
OF THE GENEALOGY OF CHRIST

The book of Ruth is also an important part of the genealogy of Christ (Matt. 1:5), which is the record that concerns the incarnation of Christ.

In the whole universe, there is nothing greater than the incarnation of Christ. After the eternal God created man, He was nearly silent for four thousand years. During that time no one knew what God was doing. The angels did not know, and the men in the Old Testament, such as Abraham, Moses, and David, did not know. Then the eternal God came out of eternity and entered into time. He came out of eternity with His divinity in order to enter into humanity to make Himself, the Divine, one with man, the human, to become a God-man. This is the greatest thing in the entire universe. The short

book of Ruth, containing only four chapters, is related in a
particular way to the incarnation of Christ.

III. THE WRITER

According to the contents of Ruth, its writer should be
Samuel, as is the case also with the book of Judges.

IV. THE TIME

According to the word "Jesse begot David" (4:22), the time
of writing must have been after the rule of the judges and in
the time of the kings. The time of the history covered in this
book comprises eleven years, from about 1322 B.C. (1:4) to
about 1312 B.C. (4:13).

V. THE PLACE

The history recorded in the book of Ruth took place in
Moab and Judah (1:1, 22).

VI. THE CONTENT

The content of this book concerns a Moabitess, Ruth. Ruth
belonged to the tribe of Moab (v. 4). Moab was the son of
Lot, the fruit of Lot's incestuous union with his daughter
(Gen. 19:30-38). According to Deuteronomy 23:3 the Moabites
were forbidden to enter the congregation of the Lord, even
to the tenth generation. Thus, as a Moabitess, Ruth was an
excluded one. Nevertheless, she was brought into the holy
elect of God and became an important ancestor of Christ
through her marriage with Boaz, the great-grandfather of
King David (Ruth 4:21-22; Matt. 1:5-6), which became a factor
that ushered in the incarnation of Christ (Matt. 1:5-16). From
this we see that Ruth became an important ancestor to bring
Christ into humanity. This ushered in the marvelous incarnation, which made God one with man. This is the intrinsic
significance of the content of the book of Ruth.

VII. THE CENTRAL THOUGHT

The central thought of the book of Ruth is that a Gentile,
even a Moabitess, could be joined to God's holy elect and
become an heir to partake of the holy inheritance through her

union with the one of the holy elect who redeemed her. This is not merely a type but a complete prefigure of the Gentile sinners' being brought, with Israel, God's elect, into the divine inheritance through the redemption of Christ in their union with Him.

VIII. THE SECTIONS

The book of Ruth has six sections.

A. Elimelech's Swerving from the Rest in God's Economy

The first section (1:1-2) shows us that Elimelech, one of God's elect, swerved from the rest in God's economy.

B. Naomi's Returning to the Rest in God's Economy

The second section (1:3-7, 19-22) concerns Naomi's returning to the rest in God's economy. Whereas Elimelech swerved from this rest, Naomi returned to it.

C. Ruth's Choosing for Her Goal

Some expositors speak of Ruth's resolution or determination. What we see in Ruth, however, is not just her resolution or her determination but her choosing for her goal. This is described in the third section of the book (1:8-18).

D. Ruth's Exercising of Her Right

The next section of this book (ch. 2) covers Ruth's exercising of her right. After she made a choice regarding her goal, she exercised her right.

E. Ruth's Seeking for Her Rest

The fifth section of this book (ch. 3) covers Ruth's seeking for her rest. Once she exercised the right that came to her through her choosing for her goal, Ruth, in wisdom, sought for her rest.

F. Ruth's Reward for God's Economy

Because Ruth was absolute for God's economy, she received a reward from God. Ruth's reward for God's economy is covered in chapter four, the last section of this book.

LIFE-STUDY OF RUTH

MESSAGE TWO

ELIMELECH'S SWERVING, NAOMI'S RETURNING, AND RUTH'S CHOOSING

Scripture Reading: Ruth 1

In this message we will consider Ruth 1, a chapter that covers Elimelech's swerving, Naomi's returning, and Ruth's choosing.

I. ELIMELECH'S SWERVING FROM THE REST IN GOD'S ECONOMY

In verses 1 and 2 we see that Elimelech swerved from the rest in God's economy. He was in the good land and had a portion of it, and he should have remained there. Remaining in the good land that God has promised and given is the real rest. Elimelech foolishly swerved from this wonderful rest.

A. Israel Living in the God-promised Land for the Carrying Out of God's Economy

Israel, as God's elect, was living in the God-promised land for the carrying out of God's economy. This means that staying in the good land is not just for us to earn a living but for us to participate in the carrying out of God's economy.

B. Israel's Rest Being Related to Their Situation with God in His Economy

Israel's rest, their prosperity for their enjoyment and their contentment, was related to their situation with God in His economy. For an Israelite to leave the good land meant that he was cutting himself off from God's eternal economy.

The book of Ruth speaks of Christ being brought into

mankind through incarnation. This is the real rest. Ruth is thus a book of rest. As we will see, after Ruth married Boaz, they brought forth a child, Obed, and Ruth enjoyed a rest with an absolute satisfaction and full expectation for her descendants. The following generations enjoyed rest under David. Then after one thousand years, they enjoyed the real rest with the Lord Jesus. Two thousand years later, this rest will be enjoyed in a fuller way in the millennial kingdom with Christ as the King. After the millennium, the enjoyment of this rest will consummate in the New Jerusalem in the new heaven and new earth for eternity. This matter of rest is the key to the book of Ruth.

C. From Bethlehem in Judah

Elimelech's mistake was to swerve from the ground, the standing, which gave him the opportunity to enjoy the rest in the good land. He swerved from Bethlehem in Judah.

1. Bethlehem, the City of David

Bethlehem, the city of David, was designated as the birthplace of the coming Christ (Micah 5:2; Luke 2:4-7). In the eyes of God, Bethlehem was a very special place, for it was the place where He, through incarnation, would be born to be a man.

2. Judah

Judah was the land of the royal tribe among Israel (Gen. 49:8-10). Of all the tribes, no tribe had a higher allotment of the land than Judah. It was the top part of the God-promised land (Exo. 3:8b), the top part of the good land (Deut. 8:7-10), and the top part of the land of Immanuel (Isa. 8:8). How mistaken Elimelech was in swerving from this land!

D. To Moab

Elimelech swerved from Bethlehem in Judah to Moab, a place of incest rejected and condemned by God. Moab was a country of the descendants of Lot through his incest (Gen. 19:30-38). It was also a country of the people who were not allowed to enter into the assembly of Jehovah because of the incest of their forefathers (Deut. 23:2-3) and because of their mistreatment of Israel (v. 4). Furthermore, Moab was a country of people whose peace and prosperity God would not allow Israel to seek all their days forever (v. 6). Finally, Moab was a country of idolatry (Judg. 10:6).

E. In the Days of the Rule of the Judges

Elimelech left in the days of the rule of the judges, under Israel's forsaking of God and under their degradation, confusion, and corruption.

F. Due to a Famine in the Good Land

Elimelech left due to a famine in the good land, a lacking of life supply for living and satisfaction as a punishment of God (Lev. 26:26; Ezek. 14:13). We may wonder how there could be a famine in the good land since God had promised that it would be a land flowing with milk and honey. God sent a famine to His people as a serious punishment. He punished them by stopping their food supply. Because they had forsaken Him as their source and Husband and had gone to idols, He let them go to their idols for food as well. There was no food from God and no food from the illegal husband of their harlotry.

G. With His Wife and Two Sons

Elimelech left the good land with his wife and two sons, who were good for the increase of the kingdom of God.

H. God's Chastisement
in Moab over the House of Elimelech

Ruth 1:3 and 5 speak of God's chastisement over the house of Elimelech. Elimelech was punished by God with death upon himself and his two sons. This left his wife, Naomi, as a widow with two daughters-in-law in a foreign country. That was the pitiful result of Elimelech's swerving from the rest in God's eternal economy.

II. NAOMI'S RETURNING TO THE REST IN GOD'S ECONOMY

In verses 4 through 7 and 19 through 22 we see Naomi's returning to the rest in God's economy.

A. From Moab

Naomi returned from Moab, the country of idolatry.

B. To Judah

Naomi returned to Judah, the land of Immanuel.

C. Having Been Stripped by God of Her Husband and of Her Two Sons

Naomi returned because she had been stripped by God first of her husband and then of her two sons, leaving her and her two daughters-in-law as widows without children (vv. 5, 20-21). Naomi returned also because she had heard that Jehovah had visited His people by giving them food (v. 6). In the Lord's recovery, we also have experienced the Lord's merciful visitation. During the last several years He has blessed us and supplied us with rich food.

D. With Ruth, Her Daughter-in-law

Naomi returned with Ruth, her daughter-in-law given to her by God for the accomplishment of His economy concerning Christ (v. 22a).

E. Arriving at Bethlehem

Naomi arrived at Bethlehem, the birthplace of the coming Christ (vv. 19a, 22b).

F. All the City Being Stirred

All the city was stirred because of Naomi and Ruth, and the women said, "Is this Naomi?" (v. 19b). Naomi said to them, "Do not call me Naomi [meaning 'my pleasantness']; call me Mara [meaning 'bitterness']; for the All-sufficient One has dealt very bitterly with me. I went out full, but Jehovah has brought me back empty. Why do you call me Naomi, when

Jehovah has afflicted me and the All-sufficient One has dealt harshly with me?" (vv. 20-21).

III. RUTH'S CHOOSING FOR HER GOAL

In verses 8 through 18 we have an account of Ruth's choosing for her goal.

A. Naomi's Proposal
to Her Two Daughters-in-law for Their Future

Naomi made a proposal to her two daughters-in-law for their future. She said to them, "Go and return, each of you, to your mother's house. May Jehovah deal kindly with you, just as you have dealt with the dead and with me. May Jehovah grant you to find rest, each of you in the house of your husband" (vv. 8-9a). Then she kissed them, and they lifted up their voice and wept, saying to her, "No, we will return with you to your people" (vv. 9b-10). Naomi told them to return and then asked them, "Why should you go with me? Do I still have sons in my womb, that they may be your husbands? Return, my daughters, go; for I am too old to have a husband. If I said, I have hope; even if I had a husband tonight and even bore sons; would you then wait until they were grown? Would you then refrain from having a husband? No, my daughters; it has been far more bitter for me than it should be for you, for the hand of Jehovah has gone forth against me" (vv. 11-13). When the daughters-in-law heard this, they lifted up their voice and wept again. Then Orpah kissed her mother-in-law, but Ruth clung to her. Naomi said to Ruth, "Your sister-in-law has now returned to her people and to her gods; return with your sister-in-law" (vv. 14-15).

B. Ruth's Choosing to Go with Naomi

Ruth said to Naomi, "Do not entreat me to leave you and turn away from following after you. For wherever you go, I will go, and wherever you dwell, I will dwell; and your people will be my people, and your God will be my God. Where you die, I will die; and there will I be buried. Jehovah do so to me, and more as well, if anything but death parts me from you" (vv. 16-17). When Naomi saw that Ruth was determined to go with her, she ceased speaking to her about it (v. 18).

Ruth chose the goal of participating with God's elect in the enjoyment of Christ, and she even became a top ancestor of Christ who helped bring forth Christ into mankind. This was more than just a resolution on the part of the Moabite widow; it was a goal, a choosing. Ruth chose God and His kingdom for the carrying out of God's economy concerning Christ. Hallelujah for such a goal and for such a person choosing this goal!

LIFE-STUDY OF RUTH

MESSAGE THREE

RUTH'S EXERCISING OF HER RIGHT

Scripture Reading: Ruth 2

After Ruth's husband died, she had two choices: remain in Moab or go with Naomi to be a foreigner in Israel. Ruth chose to go to the land of Israel because she probably had heard a great deal concerning God, God's promise, and the good land. She had heard the good news sufficiently for her to make a wonderful choice. After arriving in the land of Israel with Naomi, Ruth exercised her right. This matter is covered in chapter two.

I. GOD'S COMMANDMENT TO ISRAEL THAT TAKES CARE OF THE NEEDY ONES AMONG HIS ELECT CONCERNING THE REAPING OF THEIR HARVEST

God's commandment concerning the reaping of the harvest was that Jehovah would bless the children of Israel if they left the corners of their fields and the gleanings for the poor, the sojourners, the orphans, and the widows. Concerning this, Leviticus 23:22 says, "When you reap the harvest of your land, you shall not completely reap the corners of your field, neither shall you gather the gleanings of your harvest; you shall leave them for the poor and for the alien." A similar word is found in Leviticus 19:9-10. Deuteronomy 24:19 says, "When you reap your harvest in your field and you forget a sheaf in the field, you shall not turn back to gather it; it shall be for the sojourner, the orphan, and the widow, in order that Jehovah your God may bless you in all your undertakings." This shows not only the lovingkindness of God and how great, fine, and detailed He is, but shows also the rich produce of the good land.

God wanted to bless the harvest of the Israelites in the

good land, but this blessing had a condition—that something would be left for the poor. The people would not be allowed to reap completely the corners of their field. However, in the ordinance of the law given by God through Moses regarding reaping, the size of the corners of the field was not specified. The size depended on the landlord's faith in Jehovah. The larger one's faith in Jehovah was, the larger the corners of the field would be. I believe that it was the practice of Boaz to obey this ordinance. He must have had great faith in Jehovah. Under God's sovereignty this ordinance seems to have been written for one person—Ruth.

II. NAOMI RETURNING TO BETHLEHEM WITH HER DAUGHTER-IN-LAW RUTH AT THE BEGINNING OF THE BARLEY HARVEST

Naomi returned to Bethlehem with her daughter-in-law Ruth at the beginning of the barley harvest (Ruth 1:22b). Barley, which ripens earlier than other grains, typifies the resurrected Christ (John 6:9-10, 56-58).

III. NAOMI HAVING A RELATIVE OF HER HUSBAND'S, A MAN OF GREAT WEALTH, BY THE NAME OF BOAZ

"Now Naomi had a relative of her husband's, a man of great wealth, from Elimelech's family; and his name was Boaz" (Ruth 2:1). God is sovereign, and in His sovereignty He brought Ruth from Moab to the city of Bethlehem. Before she arrived there, He had prepared a rich, generous man by the name of Boaz.

IV. RUTH GAINING NAOMI'S PERMISSION TO GO GLEANING

Ruth gained Naomi's permission to go gleaning (vv. 2-3). Ruth asked Naomi to let her go to the field and glean among the ears of grain after him in whose sight Ruth had found favor. Naomi told Ruth to go, and she went and gleaned in the field after the reapers, happening to glean in a portion of the field belonging to Boaz.

V. BOAZ BECOMING ACQUAINTED WITH RUTH

Boaz eventually became acquainted with Ruth (vv. 4-7).

He came from Bethlehem and said to the reapers, "Jehovah be with you," and they said to him, "Jehovah bless you" (v. 4). When Boaz asked the young man who was set over the reapers concerning Ruth, the young man told him that she was the young Moabite woman who had returned with Naomi from the country of Moab and who had asked to glean and gather after the reapers among the sheaves. His word to Boaz regarding Ruth indicates that he was happy with her, considering her a woman of fidelity and virtue.

VI. BOAZ'S WORD OF GRACE TO RUTH

In verses 8 through 13 we have Boaz's word of grace to Ruth. He said to her, "Do not go to glean in another field, and also do not pass from here but stay close to my young women. Keep your eyes on the field that they reap; follow after them. I have charged my young men not to touch you. And when you are thirsty, you shall go to the vessels and drink of what the young men have drawn" (vv. 8-9). When Ruth heard these words, she fell upon her face, bowed herself to the ground, and asked Boaz, "Why have I found favor in your sight that you regard me, though I am a foreigner?" (v. 10). Boaz replied that all that she had done for her mother-in-law since the death of her husband Elimelech had been made known to him. He also had learned how she had left her father and mother and the land of her birth and had come to a people whom she had not known before. Then he said to her, "May Jehovah recompense your work, and may you have a full reward from Jehovah, the God of Israel, under whose wings you have come to take refuge" (v. 12). In response, Ruth asked that she would find favor in his sight, for he had comforted her and had spoken kindly to her (v. 13).

VII. BOAZ'S GENEROSITY TOWARD RUTH

Boaz not only spoke kindly to Ruth but also showed generosity to her (vv. 14-16). At mealtime Boaz told her to eat some food, extending some parched grain to her, and she ate and was satisfied. When she rose up to glean, Boaz charged his young men to let her glean among the standing grain and not to rebuke her. Then he went on to say to them,

"Also pull out some from the bundles for her, and leave it for her to glean; and do not rebuke her" (v. 16).

VIII. RUTH TELLING THE STORY TO NAOMI

Upon returning from the field, Ruth told the story of her experience with Boaz to Naomi, her mother-in-law (vv. 17-21). When Ruth told Naomi that she had gleaned in the field of Boaz, Naomi said to her, "Blessed be he of Jehovah, whose lovingkindness has not failed for the living and for the dead" (v. 20a). Then Naomi told Ruth that the man was close to them, one of their kinsmen (v. 20b).

IX. NAOMI CHARGING RUTH

In verse 22 Naomi charged Ruth, saying, "It is good, my daughter, that you go out with his young women, so that others do not meet you in any other field." As we will see when we come to chapter three, what was on Naomi's heart was not only that Ruth would partake of Boaz's riches and be satisfied, but also that she would gain Boaz himself as her husband and bring forth a son for the name of Elimelech.

X. RUTH STAYING CLOSE TO BOAZ'S YOUNG WOMEN

Ruth stayed close to Boaz's young women and gleaned until the end of the barley harvest and the wheat harvest; and she dwelt with her mother-in-law (v. 23).

XI. RUTH EXERCISING HER RIGHT
TO PARTAKE OF THE RICH PRODUCE
OF THE INHERITANCE OF GOD'S ELECT

In all this Ruth, as one who had returned to God from her heathen background, exercised her right to partake of the rich produce of the inheritance of God's elect. Ruth, a Moabitess, had come to the good land as a sojourner. According to her threefold status as a sojourner, a poor one, and a widow, she exercised her right to glean the harvest. Although she was poor, she never became a beggar. Her gleaning was not her begging; it was her right.

The book of Ruth portrays the way, the position, the qualification, and the right of sinners to participate in Christ and to enjoy Christ. According to God's ordination, we have been qualified and positioned to claim our right to enjoy Christ. This means that today we do not need to beg God to save us. We can go to God to claim His salvation for ourselves. We have the position, the qualification, and the right to claim salvation from God. This is the highest standard of receiving the gospel.

XII. TYPES IMPLIED IN THIS AROMATIC STORY

As a narration, the book of Ruth is lovely, touching, convincing, and subduing. In the aromatic story in chapter two, four types are implied.

A. Boaz, Rich in Wealth

Boaz, rich in wealth (2:1), typifies Christ, who is rich in the divine grace (2 Cor. 12:9).

B. The Field of the God-promised Good Land

The field of the God-promised good land (Ruth 2:2-3) typifies the all-inclusive Christ, who is the source of all the spiritual and divine products for the life supply to God's elect (Phil. 1:19b).

C. Barley and Wheat

Barley and wheat (Ruth 2:23) typify Christ as the material for making food for both God and His people (Lev. 2; John 6:9, 33, 35).

D. Ruth, a Moabitess, a Heathen Sinner

Ruth, a Moabitess (Deut. 23:3), a heathen sinner, alienated from God's promises (Eph. 2:12), given the right to partake of the gleaning of the harvest of God's elect typifies the "Gentile dogs" who are privileged to partake of the crumbs under the table of the portion of God's elect children (Col. 1:12; Matt. 15:25-28).

LIFE-STUDY OF RUTH

MESSAGE FOUR

RUTH'S SEEKING FOR HER REST

Scripture Reading: Ruth 3

Chapter one shows Ruth's choosing, chapter two shows Ruth's exercising of her right, and chapter three shows Ruth's seeking for her rest. We need to enjoy Christ to such an extent that we have rest. In order to have rest, we surely need a home. No place can give us as much rest as our home. In chapter three Naomi proposed and even pushed to gain a home for Ruth.

The steps taken by Ruth correspond to our spiritual experience. Before we were saved, we all had our own taste and choice. Under the Lord's sovereign arrangement, we heard the gospel and made a resolution to become a believer of Christ. Our choice was to believe in Christ. By believing in the Lord Jesus, we were organically joined to Him. Now He is in us and we are in Him. With this intimate, organic union, we must begin to pursue Christ in order to gain, possess, experience, and enjoy Him. This is typified by Ruth's exercising of her right to gain and possess the produce of the good land. Just as Ruth had the right to enjoy the produce of the good land after coming into the land, so we have the right to enjoy Christ as our good land after believing in Him.

It is a tragedy that Christianity, both Catholicism and Protestantism, has not seen this matter of enjoying Christ. The Lord Jesus said, "He who eats Me, he also shall live because of Me" (John 6:57). Our Savior can be eaten; He is our heavenly food and manna. According to Revelation 2, whoever overcomes may eat of Christ as the tree of life and as the hidden manna (vv. 7, 17). The Bible reveals that Christ is not only our food but also our drink, clothing, and breath. He is our daily necessities. Every day we need to enjoy Him.

We must be like Ruth and exercise our right to enjoy Christ. Every morning we should "glean" from the "field" of the Bible.

However, after our gleaning we still need a home so that we can have a settled rest. This kind of rest can come only through marriage. In Ruth 3:1 Naomi said to Ruth, "My daughter, I must seek some resting place for you." Naomi wanted to find a way to establish a home for Ruth. If Ruth was to have a home for her rest, she needed a husband. Naomi realized that the proper person to be Ruth's husband was Boaz, who typifies Christ.

I realize that many of us love the Lord Jesus, but have we taken Him as our Husband? Have you ever had a time with the Lord when you said, "Lord, You are my Husband"? Even though you are saved and you love the Lord, you will not have a home for your rest until you marry the Lord Jesus, taking Him as your Husband.

In these messages on Joshua, Judges, and Ruth, the Lord has given us a clear view of how we should take Christ as our unique Husband. After the people of Israel entered the good land under Joshua, there was a history of miserable chaos because Israel was not faithful. She left God as her Husband to go to many husbands, to many idols. In this modern age there are many idols, such as entertainment, sports, and shopping, which cause Christians to be unfaithful. It seems as if they have never been married to Christ, that they have never actually taken Him as their Husband. As a consequence, they are roaming, wandering from place to place with no rest.

The place to find our Husband is in our home, the church. Christ is the Husband in the church. To have a husband is not sufficient. We must also have a home. Without a home we have no rest. If we have Christ, enjoy Christ, and experience Christ, yet we do not have the church, we are still homeless. Therefore, we must stress not only Christ as our Husband but also the church as our home. Christ as our Husband and the church as our home are a complete unit for us to have a proper and adequate rest.

Ruth was enjoying her life with Naomi, but Naomi was

clear that Ruth needed to be married to Boaz. Although according to God's law the Jews and the Moabites were to be separated, in His sovereignty God had a way to bring Ruth, a Moabitess, and Boaz together. By the time of chapter three, Ruth and Boaz had already met in the field where Ruth was gleaning, and they were prepared, qualified, and ready to be married. I believe that Boaz loved Ruth and that she loved him. But this love was entirely inward, with no outward expression. Since this was the situation, there was the need for Naomi, as the person in the middle, to push Ruth and Boaz to get married.

My burden today is like Naomi's. I am seeking a resting place for you, and the only way for you to have rest is to take Christ as your Husband. Thus, I am here as a person in the middle to push you to marry Christ. I am quite concerned that you have never known Christ as your Husband and that you have not yet found a home for your rest. You may know Christ as your Redeemer, Savior, Master, and Lord. You may even know that He is your food, drink, breath, and clothing. But do you know Him as your Husband? Perhaps you glean daily in His field and recognize Him as the Landlord. You need to do more than to glean in His field—you need to take Him as your Husband. My burden, therefore, is to push all of us to marry Christ. I am pushing us to marry Christ so that we can build up a home and enjoy Him in this home, which is the church.

Nothing is more intimate than marriage. Taking Christ as our Husband is a most intimate matter. If we marry Christ, taking Him as our Husband, our life will be changed. We will realize that we must have a wife's fidelity, and we will learn how to enjoy Christ as our life, walking and behaving in oneness with Him. Then we will become those who gain Christ and enjoy Christ, loving Him, staying at home with Him, and living with Him at home, in the church. If we do this, we will truly know the church life in the Lord's recovery.

Now that we have seen the intrinsic significance of chapter three of Ruth, let us consider this chapter in more detail.

I. PROMOTED BY HER MOTHER-IN-LAW

In 3:1-5 we see that Ruth's seeking for her rest was promoted by her mother-in-law Naomi.

A. To Seek Some Resting Place for Ruth

In verse 1 Naomi said to Ruth, "My daughter, I must seek some resting place for you, that it may go well with you."

B. Instructing Ruth What to Do

Naomi instructed Ruth what to do (vv. 2-4). She told Ruth to wash herself, anoint herself, put on her best clothes, and go down to the threshing floor where Boaz, their relative, was winnowing the barley. She further instructed Ruth not to make herself known to the man until he had finished eating and drinking. Then Naomi told her to notice the place where he lies down and go there, uncover his feet, and lie down. Naomi concluded by telling her that Boaz would tell her what she should do.

C. Ruth's Obedience

Ruth was obedient to her mother-in-law, saying to her, "All that you say, I will do" (v. 5).

II. CARRIED OUT BY RUTH

A. According to Her Mother-in-law's Charge

Ruth went down to the threshing floor and did all that her mother-in-law had charged her (v. 6).

B. Approaching Boaz Based upon the God-ordained Way

Verses 7 through 9 give an account of how Ruth approached Boaz. Her approaching him was based upon the God-ordained way (4:5; Lev. 25:25; Deut. 25:5-10).

III. ACCEPTED BY BOAZ

In Ruth 3:10-15 we see that Ruth was accepted by Boaz.

A. Boaz's Promise

When Ruth identified herself and asked Boaz to spread his cloak over her, he said, "Blessed be you of Jehovah, my daughter. You have shown your latter kindness to be better than your first by not going after the choice young men, whether poor or rich" (v. 10). Then he promised to do all that she had said. He continued by explaining that although he was a kinsman, there was a kinsman closer than he. Boaz went on to say that if that other kinsman was not willing to do the kinsman's duty for Ruth, then he would do it for her.

B. Boaz's Generous Care

In verses 14 and 15 we see Boaz's generous care for Ruth.

IV. RUTH'S REPORT TO HER MOTHER-IN-LAW

According to verses 16 through 18 Ruth gave a report to her mother-in-law.

A. The Good News

Ruth reported the good news concerning all that Boaz had done for her. In particular, she spoke of the six measures of barley that he had given to her.

B. The Mother-in-law's Faith

Verse 18 reveals the mother-in-law's faith. Naomi had the faith that Boaz would not rest until he had sought rest for Ruth.

V. FOR THE CONTINUATION OF THE GENEALOGY TO BRING IN CHRIST

If we consider Matthew 1:5-6 and 16, we will see that Ruth's seeking for her rest was actually for the continuation of the genealogy to bring in Christ.

VI. THE EVALUATION OF BOAZ

Chapter three of Ruth presents a high evaluation of Boaz. This chapter indicates that he was high in morality (vv. 8-11), that he was pure in conduct (v. 14), that he was wise in decision (vv. 12-13), and that he was faithful in keeping God's ordination (Lev. 25:25; Deut. 25:5-10).

LIFE-STUDY OF RUTH

MESSAGE FIVE

RUTH'S REWARD FOR GOD'S ECONOMY

Scripture Reading: Ruth 4

In this message we will consider Ruth's reward for God's economy. We have seen that Ruth made a choice for her goal and that she exercised her right to enjoy the rich land. Under the prodding of Naomi, Ruth sought for a resting place, and finally she received a reward, a gain, for God's economy. A real seeker after God, Ruth eventually gained what she sought after. She chose her goal, she exercised her right, and she sought for a husband and a home as a resting place.

I. GAINING A REDEEMING HUSBAND

According to chapter four, there are four aspects of Ruth's reward. First, in verses 10 through 13 she gained a redeeming husband (typifying Christ as the redeeming Husband to the believers—Rom. 7:4). Ruth's gaining of such a husband was witnessed and blessed by the people and the elders in the gate (Ruth 4:11-12), and it was also blessed by God (v. 13b).

We need to be impressed with the fact that Ruth's reward was for God's economy. Man was created by God with a purpose according to His eternal economy. This economy is not a common plan or merely a small arrangement. In the universe the divine and eternal economy is second only to God Himself. According to His economy God created the heavens, the earth, and man. But God's enemy came in to attempt to break the line that joins man to God and God to man. In Genesis 3 Satan cut this line, but eventually Christ as the promised seed of the woman (v. 15) came to repair the line by redeeming man back to God.

In the books of Joshua, Judges, and Ruth, there were not many on earth who had linked themselves to God. At the time of Ruth the line between God and man was very thin. It was thin to such an extent that it consisted mainly of two persons, a couple—Boaz and Ruth. This couple was brought together in a marvelous and sovereign way. Although Boaz was born an Israelite and Ruth was born in Moab, an incestuous country, Ruth was brought to the good land, even to Bethlehem, the city of David.

Ruth had the right to glean from many different fields, but she went to Boaz's field. When Naomi, Ruth's mother-in-law, learned that Ruth had gleaned in Boaz's field, she was very happy. Desiring to find a resting place for Ruth, Naomi instructed her about what to do (3:2-4). Ruth followed Naomi's direction, and she and Boaz were brought into a courtship. When they were at the threshing floor, she applied to be his wife. He said to her, "All that you say, I will do for you; for all the assembly of my people know that you are a worthy woman. And now it is true that I am a kinsman, yet there is a kinsman closer than I. Stay for the night; and in the morning if he will do the kinsman's duty, fine; let him do it. But if he is not willing to do the kinsman's duty for you, I will do it for you, as Jehovah lives" (vv. 11-13). In a very kind way Boaz was indicating that he would act in accordance with God's ordinances (Lev. 25:25; Deut. 25:5-10). Their courtship led to their marriage. Through that marriage Ruth, a Moabite widow, gained the holy citizens' citizenship, becoming one among God's elect.

The crucial point here is that, as part of her reward for God's economy, Ruth gained a redeeming husband, who typifies Christ as the redeeming Husband to the believers. Only Christ can be both our Husband and our Redeemer. Before we were saved, we were in trouble and could not get out of trouble. Now as believers in Christ, we have a Husband who is our eternal, present, and daily Redeemer, rescuing us, saving us, delivering us, from all our troubles. What a gain this is!

II. REDEEMED FROM THE INDEBTEDNESS
OF THE DEAD HUSBAND

In addition to gaining a redeeming husband, Ruth was

redeemed from the indebtedness of the dead husband (Ruth 4:1-9). This typifies being redeemed from the sin of the believers' old man. Ruth's dead husband had sold his field, and the indebtedness of that transaction had fallen upon her in the marriage union and needed to be redeemed. Boaz said to the kinsman who was closer than he, "On the day you buy the field from Naomi's hand, you must also acquire Ruth the Moabitess, the wife of the dead man, in order to raise up the dead man's name upon his inheritance" (v. 5). That kinsman replied, "I cannot redeem it for myself, or else it will mar my own inheritance. Redeem for yourself what I should redeem, for I cannot redeem it" (v. 6). Boaz did so, redeeming Ruth from her indebtedness.

Our Husband, Christ, is not merely capable; He is almighty. He has redeemed us from the indebtedness of our dead husband. According to Romans 7 the dead husband, our old husband, is our old man. God created us to be His wife, but we rebelled against Him. We gave Him up and assumed the position of the husband for ourselves. Our sinful husband encumbered us with many debts. But on the day we married Christ, we received a Husband who is our almighty, omnipotent Redeemer. We all need Christ to be such a Husband to us. Having Him as our Husband, we should come to Him and simply say, "Lord Jesus, I need You."

III. BECOMING A CRUCIAL ANCESTOR IN THE GENEALOGY TO BRING IN THE ROYAL HOUSE OF DAVID FOR THE PRODUCING OF CHRIST

Another aspect of Ruth's reward is that she became a crucial ancestor in the genealogy to bring in the royal house of David for the producing of Christ (Ruth 4:13b-22; Matt. 1:5-16). This indicates that she had an all-inclusive and all-extensive gain with the position and capacity to bring Christ into the human race. She is thus a great link in the chain that is bringing Christ to every corner of the earth. We all are indebted to Ruth, for without her Christ could not have reached us. But wherever we may be on earth, Christ has reached us through Ruth.

The burden of this ministry is to produce Christ in the believers. This means that the goal of this ministry is not to teach you to be humble or merely to glorify God in your behavior. Rather, the goal of this ministry is to "inject" you with Christ, to impart Christ as an "antibiotic" to you. The more we receive such an injection, the more we will be able to sing, "Christ liveth in me, / Christ liveth in me; / Oh! what a salvation this, / That Christ liveth in me" (*Hymns,* #507). On the one hand, this injection of Christ will kill our old man; on the other hand, it will make us producers of Christ, those who minister Christ to others.

IV. TO CONTINUE THE LINE
OF THE GOD-CREATED HUMANITY
FOR THE INCARNATION OF CHRIST

Ruth not only became a crucial ancestor in the genealogy for the producing of Christ, but she also continued the line of the God-created humanity for the incarnation of Christ (Matt. 1:5-16). The incarnation of Christ was a matter of His being brought out of eternity into time with His divinity. In a practical way, this needs to take place in our daily living. Every day of our Christian life should be a continuation of Christ's incarnation, with Christ being brought forth in order to be born into others through our ministering Christ to them. In order for this to happen, we all need to speak for Christ, to speak forth Christ, and even speak Christ to others. Ministering Christ in this way will surely change us.

V. FIRST SAMUEL TO MALACHI
BEING A LONG RECORD OF THE GENERATIONS
FOR THE PROLONGED LINE OF HUMANITY
FOR CHRIST'S INCARNATION

First Samuel to Malachi is a long record of the generations for the prolonged line of humanity for Christ's incarnation (Matt. 1:17).

LIFE-STUDY OF RUTH

BOAZ AND RUTH
TYPIFYING CHRIST AND THE CHURCH

Scripture Reading: Ruth 2:1, 14-16; 3:15; 4:9-10, 13

In these messages on Joshua, Judges, and Ruth, my emphasis has been on our gaining Christ, experiencing Christ, and enjoying Christ so that we may be the church. In this message we will consider how Boaz and Ruth typify Christ and the church. Boaz is a type of Christ, and Ruth is a type not only of the seeking saints but of the church. Ultimately, Ruth typifies the church.

I. BOAZ TYPIFYING CHRIST

A. Two Prominent Persons Typifying Christ

At the beginning and at the end of the portion of Israel's history from Joshua to Ruth are two prominent persons typifying Christ (Josh. 1:1; Ruth 4:21). These persons are Joshua and Boaz, who signify two aspects of one person.

1. Joshua at the Beginning

At the beginning Joshua typifies Christ in bringing God's chosen people into God's ordained blessings (Josh. 1:2-4; Eph. 1:3-14). As typified by Joshua, Christ has brought us into the good land, has taken possession of the land for us, and has allotted the land to us as our inheritance for our enjoyment. Christ has gained the good land for us, and eventually He is the good land for us to enjoy.

2. Boaz at the End

At the end Boaz typifies Christ in other aspects. In particular, he typifies Christ as our Husband for our satisfaction.

B. The Aspects in Which Boaz Typifies Christ

Boaz typifies Christ in two aspects.

1. As a Man Rich in Wealth and Generous in Giving

As a man, rich in wealth and generous in giving (Ruth 2:1, 14-16; 3:15), Boaz typifies Christ, whose divine riches are unsearchable and who takes care of God's needy people with His bountiful supply (Eph. 3:8; 2 Cor. 12:9; Phil. 1:19b).

Sadly, in their experience many of today's Christians do not have Christ in His riches, and they do not have Him as the Husband. In the church we have Christ as our riches, and we also have Him as our Husband. In Ephesians Paul speaks of the unsearchable riches of Christ (3:8). He speaks also of Christ as the Husband of the church (5:23-32). In Revelation our Husband is unveiled as the Lamb, the redeeming God (21:2, 9). The Bible reveals, therefore, that Christ with His unsearchable riches is our Husband. In the last two chapters of the Bible, we see that Christ, the Lamb, is our Husband and that we, the believers in Christ, are the Lamb's wife.

2. As a Kinsman of Mahlon

As a kinsman of Mahlon, the dead husband of Ruth, who redeemed the lost right of Mahlon's property and took Mahlon's widow, Ruth, as his wife for the producing of the needed heirs (Ruth 4:9-10, 13), Boaz typifies Christ in redeeming the church and making the church His counterpart for His increase (Eph. 5:23-32; John 3:29-30).

II. RUTH TYPIFYING THE CHURCH

A. Ruth, Being a Woman in Adam in God's Creation and a Moabitess in Man's Fall, Thus Becoming an Old Man with These Two Aspects

Ruth, being a woman in Adam in God's creation and a Moabitess in man's fall, thus becoming an old man with these two aspects, typifies the church, before her salvation, as men in God's creation and sinners in man's fall being "our old man" (Rom. 6:6). Ruth became a Moabitess not *because* of man's fall but *in* man's fall. The Moabites, an incestuous people, typify all sinners, because all sinners were born of incest (John 8:41, 44a). This means that Ruth was not the only one with an incestuous background. We all have the same background. Adam and Eve joined themselves to Satan; that is, they married Satan. As human beings created by God, we should have married our Creator, taking Him as our Husband (Isa. 54:5), but instead we married a fellow creature, Satan. This is incest.

B. Ruth, Being a Widow Redeemed by Boaz, Who Cleared the Indebtedness of Her Dead Husband for the Recovery of the Lost Right of Her Dead Husband's Property

Ruth, being the widow of the dead husband, redeemed by Boaz, who cleared the indebtedness of her dead husband for the recovery of the lost right of her dead husband's property, typifies the church with her old man as her crucified husband (Rom. 7:4a) redeemed by Christ, who cleared away her old man's sin for the recovery of the lost right of her fallen natural man created by God.

We need to realize that the believers' old man consists of a natural part created by God and a fallen part corrupted by sin. In God's creation we are good—we are "doves"; but in the fallen Adam we are evil—we are "serpents." The natural part is good and desires to do what is good, whereas the fallen part practices what is evil (Rom. 7:19, 21). From this we see that in the old man typified by Ruth, we have two natures and that one of these natures is good and the other is evil. The evil nature, acting with the good one, assumed to be the husband, and together they became the old man, our incestuous husband.

Our old man has been crucified with Christ (Rom. 6:6). Christ's crucifixion destroyed the fallen part of our old man, but it redeemed the created part. Christ did not redeem the fallen part of our old man; on the contrary, He terminated it. However, He redeemed our created part in order to recover us.

Therefore, Christ's death on the cross terminated the fallen part of our old man and redeemed the part created by God.

C. Ruth, after Being Redeemed by Boaz, Becoming a New Wife to Him

Ruth, after being redeemed by Boaz, becoming a new wife to him typifies the church, after being saved, through the regeneration of the church's natural man, becoming the counterpart of Christ (Rom. 7:4b). Just as the redeemed Ruth became a new wife to Boaz, so the saved and regenerated church has become His new wife, His counterpart, in the organic union with Him.

D. Ruth Being United with Boaz

Ruth being united to Boaz typifies the Gentile sinners being attached to Christ that they may partake of the inheritance of God's promise (Eph. 3:6).

The more we consider these aspects of Ruth as a type of the church, the more we can know our status as believers in Christ today. First, we were created by God. Second, we became fallen persons. Third, we were redeemed by Christ. Fourth, we were regenerated by the pneumatic Christ as the life-giving Spirit. Thus, we may summarize our status in four words: created, fallen, redeemed, and regenerated.

Let us now consider further how, in typology, the various aspects of Ruth's situation apply to us today. In God's creation Ruth was good, but she became fallen in Adam. When she turned to Israel, she believed in the saving God and was redeemed. Then, having become a new person, she married Boaz and became his new wife.

As signified by the type of Ruth and her dead husband, Ruth's natural part created by God and her fallen part cooperated to assume to be the husband, forsaking God as the Husband. This husband was the main part of her old man, which was composed of her God-created part and her fallen part. The old man as the illegal husband made many mistakes and incurred a great deal of debt, thereby selling himself and losing his right as a God-created being because of his sins. After Ruth's husband died, she was not only a widow but was also in a condition of indebtedness. The only way out of this condition was to be united in marriage to the proper person. When Ruth married Boaz, she was redeemed from her indebtedness, and she became his new wife for the producing of the needed heirs.

This is a picture of our situation today. Christ, our Husband, died to redeem us and to clear the indebtedness caused by the sins of our old man. Then in resurrection He, as the life-giving Spirit, regenerated us to make us, as created, fallen, and redeemed persons, a new creation married to Him. Now, in the organic union between Christ and us, we can bring forth Christ and spread Christ for His increase.

At this juncture, I would ask you to note the following five matters related to Ruth typifying the church. I hope that these matters will help us to grasp the intrinsic significance of Ruth as a type of the church.

1. The believers' old man is composed of two parts: the natural part created by God and the fallen part corrupted by sin. This old man of ours has been crucified with Christ. This crucifixion of Christ has redeemed our natural created part and destroyed our fallen part and cleared our sin caused by this fallen part.

2. Our natural man was created by God to be God's counterpart taking God as our Husband and Head, but in our fall our natural man put God aside and made himself our husband and head, thus becoming the main part of our old man.

3. After being redeemed and regenerated, our natural man, not including our fallen part, becomes our new man and takes Christ as our new Husband in the divine organic union with Him (Rom. 7:4).

4. Ruth's old husband typifies our fallen part of our old man, and his indebtedness typifies our sin caused by our fallen part. Ruth herself typifies our natural man created by God and redeemed and regenerated to be the new man as the counterpart of Christ.

5. The first kinsman of Ruth's husband typifies our natural man who cannot and will not redeem us from the indebtedness (sin) of our old man. Boaz, the second kinsman

of Ruth's husband, typifies Christ, who partook of blood and flesh (Heb. 2:14) to be our Kinsman and who can redeem us from our sin, recover the lost right of our natural man in God's creation, be our new Husband in His divine organic union with us, and take us for His counterpart for His increase.

Some may say that Christ has redeemed our fallen man, but this kind of speaking is ambiguous. Actually, Christ will not redeem anything that is fallen. Within fallen man is a part that was created by God and that can still be used by Him. Christ redeemed this God-created part of the old man, destroying the fallen part and clearing away the sin caused by this fallen part. Therefore, with respect to the believers' old man, Christ's crucifixion accomplished three things. It redeemed the God-created part of our being, it destroyed the fallen part of our being, and it cleared away our sin, which was caused by this fallen part.

Christ can be regarded as our Kinsman because He partook of blood and flesh to be a man. However, as our Kinsman He is not as close to us as our self, our natural man—our first kinsman. The natural man created by God is the first kinsman, and Christ is the second. Because the first kinsman, typified by Ruth's closest kinsman, did not have the capacity to redeem us, Christ came as the second one to redeem us, to recover our lost birthright, to become our new Husband in the divine organic union, and to take us for His counterpart for His increase.

LIFE-STUDY OF RUTH

MESSAGE SEVEN

RUTH'S STATUSES TYPIFYING
THE STATUSES OF THE BELIEVERS IN CHRIST

Scripture Reading: Ruth 1:16-17; 2:2, 11-12; 4:9-13

The book of Ruth tells us a very famous story. In this story the central role belongs to Ruth, and this role has ten statuses. Although I began to study this book more than sixty years ago and although I was taught by others regarding it, I have found it difficult to find out the various statuses of Ruth. Only recently have I seen a clear view of these statuses. In this message, therefore, I have the burden to speak a very brief word concerning Ruth's ten statuses and concerning how they are a type of the statuses of the believers in Christ today.

RUTH'S TEN STATUSES

Ruth's first status was that of a God-created person who was very good (Gen. 1:27, 31). Second, she was a fallen person in Adam who was condemned by God and constituted a sinner before God (Rom. 5:18a, 19a). Third, she became an old man to be, by forsaking God as her Husband, an old husband to herself (Rom. 6:6a; 7:2) who brought her into indebtedness. Fourth, she became a debtor in the sin of her old husband. Fifth, she was a Moabitess, an incestuous Gentile abandoned by God (Deut. 23:3). Sixth, she became one who joined God's elect, Israel, in partaking of God's promises (Eph. 2:12-13; 3:6). Seventh, she was redeemed by her kinsman, Boaz, to be a new wife to him, her new husband (Ruth 4:5, 13). Eighth, she was one who kept the line of Christ's incarnation (Matt. 1:5b). Ninth, she was the great-grandmother of David who brought forth the royal family of the God-ordained government on the earth. Tenth, she became a crucial ancestor of

Christ who brought forth Christ, the embodiment of God, to men on earth.

We may summarize Ruth's statuses by saying that she was a natural, God-created person; a fallen, corrupted person; an old wife to an old husband—a person in the old man involved with sin, with indebtedness; a person who joined God's elect; a redeemed person; a new wife; a person who brought in the royal family of the divine government on earth; and one of the crucial ancestors of Christ who brought Christ to the human race. Stated simply, Ruth was a natural person, a fallen person, a person involved in sin, a redeemed person, a person united to a new husband, and a person who brought Christ to humanity.

A TYPE OF THE BELIEVERS' STATUSES

Now we need to see that in her ten statuses Ruth typifies the believers in their statuses. First, as a God-created person with her status of a natural person with its rights by birth, Ruth typifies the believers as a natural man. Second, by her status as a fallen person—as a Moabitess, a descendant of an incestuous race—Ruth typifies the believers as the fallen man with all his corruption in nature. Third, in her status as the wife of her old husband with his indebtedness—that is, as a person involved with sin and indebted because of it—Ruth typifies the believers as the old man composed of the natural man and the fallen man. Fourth, in her status as a person redeemed by her kinsman, Ruth typifies the believers as those who have been terminated by the cross in the fallen part of their old man and redeemed back to God in the God-created part, with all the indebtedness of sin cleared up and with the birthright recovered. Fifth, in her status as the wife of Boaz in the marriage union, Ruth typifies the believers in God's new creation as parts of the new man to be the counterpart of Christ in the organic union. Sixth, in her status as an ancestor of Christ to bring forth Christ to the human race and to minister Christ to all the people on earth, Ruth typifies the believers as ministers of Christ, who bring and present Christ to all men, supplying them with Christ universally.

From the typology of Ruth's statuses, we can see that as a natural man, we became fallen and involved with sin. Because of this, we needed Christ as our Kinsman to be our Redeemer. After we were redeemed, we became a new wife to Christ, our new Husband in God's new creation. As such, we have become the ministers of Christ.

May we all be impressed with the fact that in these great things Ruth typifies us, the believers in Christ: in God's creation, in man's fall, in the old man's living, in Christ's redemption, in God's new creation, and in Christ's ministry. Today we are ministers of Christ, bringing Christ forth and ministering Christ to people everywhere.

LIFE-STUDY OF RUTH

MESSAGE EIGHT

A CONCLUDING WORD

Scripture Reading: Judg. 13:24-25; 14:6, 19; 15:14; 16:28-30; Ruth 1:16-17, 20-21; 2:10-16; 3:1, 7-13; 4:9-15

In this concluding word on the book of Ruth, I have the burden to cover a very crucial point in Joshua, Judges, and Ruth.

GOD'S MOVE IN THE SPIRIT OF POWER
AND GOD'S MOVE IN THE SPIRIT OF LIFE

This crucial point is that these books show us one picture with two sides. One side concerns God's move in His economical Spirit, the Spirit of power; the other side concerns God's move in His essential Spirit, the Spirit of life. With all the judges, and even with Joshua and Caleb, we can see only the work, the move, of God in power. In the books of Joshua and Judges it is hard to find even a hint of God's move in His life.

SAMSON AS A TYPICAL ILLUSTRATION

Samson is a typical illustration of one who moves in the Spirit of power but not in the Spirit of life. Samson was very powerful, even at the time of his death (Judg. 16:28-30), yet with him we cannot see anything of life. Yes, he was a Nazarite, keeping his hair long as a sign that he submitted to God as his Head, not drinking wine, and not eating unclean food. However, this was his following the divine regulations; it did not indicate that he had anything of the divine life. Even though Samson was a Nazarite, he did not know how to restrain the lust of his flesh. The matter of sex was a great stumbling block to him, and both among God's holy people in the Holy Land and among the Gentiles, he practiced the indulging of his lust. This shows that he was not a person in life.

Furthermore, the account of Samson, as the last judge, the conclusion of the judges, indicates that the entire situation of the judges consummated in the exercising of power without anything of life. It is difficult to understand how a Nazarite could be such a fleshly person. He was full of power and also full of lust. In his case, these two things went together.

This picture answers a question that I have had for many years. A number of Pentecostal preachers have been reckless, without any restraint, or control, of the lust of their flesh. Yet at the same time they have been genuinely powerful in their preaching. On the one hand, they powerfully preached the fundamental gospel concerning Christ, the Son of God, as our Savior; on the other hand, they were living in fornication. I have known a number of cases like this both in China and in the United States. For a long time I could not understand how there could be such a situation. Now I realize that these preachers are today's Samsons. Jehovah's Spirit came upon Samson (Judg. 13:25; 14:6, 19); there is no doubt that he had the real power of God. Nevertheless, he and so many of the judges had no control over their indulgence in lust, such as Gideon, who had seventy-two sons of many wives (8:30-31; 9:5); Jair, who had thirty sons (10:3-4); Ibzan, who had thirty sons and thirty daughters, and brought in thirty foreign daughters from abroad for his sons (12:8-9); and Abdon, who had forty sons and thirty grandsons (12:13-14).

THE BOOK OF RUTH BEING A BOOK OF LIFE

In contrast, the book of Ruth is a book not of power but of life.

The Example of Naomi

Elimelech, the husband of Naomi, was punished by God because he did not live according to God's eternal economy. He did not commit fornication; on the contrary, it seems that he just made a little mistake in leaving the Holy Land. But when he left the good land due to the famine, God came in and dealt with him, leaving his wife and his two daughters-in-law with nothing, as widows without children. I believe that before going to Moab, Elimelech mortgaged all his property, including the inheritance of his two sons. Eventually, Naomi, a widow with two widowed daughters-in-law, returned from the land of Moab, owning nothing. Nevertheless, Naomi did not rebel against God's dealing. Instead, admitting that God had dealt not only with her husband but also with her, she said, "The All-sufficient One has dealt very bitterly with me. I went out full, but Jehovah has brought me back empty" (Ruth 1:20b-21a). From her speaking we can see that she was a godly woman. She believed in God, regarded Him, and feared Him.

When Naomi came back to the Holy Land, she came back to the rest in God's economy to participate again in the enjoyment of the God-promised land, where there would be the possibility of being related to Christ's genealogy. Her returning was a great thing, yet it was not accomplished by power. Rather, she came back as a poor beggar who sent her daughter-in-law Ruth to glean in the field.

The Example of Ruth

Ruth was outstanding in life. The purpose of the book of Ruth is not to tell us anything concerning power but to reveal the things of life to the uttermost. Naomi made it clear to Ruth that she had no capacity to produce a husband for her who could redeem her and bring forth a descendant for her father-in-law, Elimelech. Feeling that the situation was hopeless, Naomi encouraged Ruth to return to her mother's house in order to have a future. Ruth's reply was full of life. She would go with Naomi forever, being with her in poverty. Ruth said to Naomi, "Do not entreat me to leave you and turn away from following after you. For wherever you go, I will go, and wherever you dwell, I will dwell; and your people will be my people, and your God will be my God. Where you die, I will die; and there will I be buried. Jehovah do so to me, and more as well, if anything but death parts me from you" (vv. 16-17). This is the real spirit of the New Testament believers—to follow Jesus by forsaking everything: parents, children, relatives, houses, and so forth (Matt. 10:37; 19:29; Mark 10:29-30; Luke 14:26). This is the way of life revealed in the New Testament.

The Example of Boaz

Like Naomi and Ruth, Boaz was a person in life to the uttermost. Naomi said to Ruth, "My daughter, I must seek some resting place for you, that it may go well with you" (Ruth 3:1). Then Naomi charged her to wash herself, anoint herself, put on her best clothes, go down to the threshing floor, and, at the proper time, make herself known to Boaz. Eventually, Ruth identified herself to Boaz, saying, "I am Ruth, your maidservant. Spread your cloak over your maidservant, for you are a kinsman" (v. 9).

In his contact with Ruth at the threshing floor that night, Boaz was absolutely restrained, not moved, in his lust, absolutely different from the lust-indulging judges. Boaz blessed Ruth and highly appraised her. Then he told her that he was willing to bear his responsibility according to God's ordinance to redeem Elimelech's inheritance, yet he would not overstep the one who was ahead of him in this matter (vv. 12-13). Here Boaz seemed to be saying, "Daughter, wait until tomorrow. Yes, I am your kinsman, and we are free in God. But there is another kinsman who is closer to you than I am, and he must be allowed to go ahead of me. If I do not care for him in this matter, the holy people of God will condemn me for overstepping. Let the other kinsman go ahead of me. If he is not willing to do the kinsman's duty for you, I will do it for you." Boaz was lawful in every way, and his being lawful was based not on power but on life. This shows that Boaz had the highest standard of life.

TAKING THE WAY OF LIFE IN THE LORD'S RECOVERY

In the Lord's recovery, should we take the way of the judges to be powerful and to do a great work? If we take the way of the judges instead of the way of life, whatever we accomplish will mean nothing. Not one judge was a forefather of Christ. The judges had nothing to do with keeping the line in humanity to bring in God in His incarnation. It was Ruth and Boaz who participated in keeping this line. However, they did not fight a war; they did not exercise any power.

It is crucial for us to see that only life can bring Christ forth. Only life can keep the lineage, maintaining the thin line to bring God into humanity, to produce Christ and to minister Christ and to supply the entire human race with Christ. This was done not by the judges but by Ruth and Boaz, who took the way of life.

In the Lord's recovery, I have very much promoted the gaining of the increase, but I do not mean that we should try to gain the increase by being a Samson or a Gideon. I would rather have no increase and keep my genuineness in life. I would rather be without any power, without any result from the work, and remain in the line that brings forth Christ out of eternity into time, that brings forth Christ with His divinity into humanity.

ABOUT THE AUTHOR

Witness Lee was born in 1905 in northern China and raised in a Christian family. At age 19 he was fully captured for Christ and immediately consecrated himself to preach the gospel for the rest of his life. Early in his service, he met Watchman Nee, a renowned preacher, teacher, and writer. Witness Lee labored together with Watchman Nee under his direction. In 1934 Watchman Nee entrusted Witness Lee with the responsibility for his publication operation, called the Shanghai Gospel Bookroom.

Prior to the Communist takeover in 1949, Witness Lee was sent by Watchman Nee and his other co-workers to Taiwan to ensure that the things delivered to them by the Lord would not be lost. Watchman Nee instructed Witness Lee to continue the former's publishing operation abroad as the Taiwan Gospel Bookroom, which has been publicly recognized as the publisher of Watchman Nee's works outside China. Witness Lee's work in Taiwan manifested the Lord's abundant blessing. From a mere 350 believers, newly fled from the mainland, the churches in Taiwan grew to 20,000 in five years.

In 1962 Witness Lee felt led of the Lord to come to the United States, settling in California. During his 35 years of service in the U.S., he ministered in weekly meetings and weekend conferences, delivering several thousand spoken messages. Much of his speaking has since been published as over 400 titles. Many of these have been translated into over fourteen languages. He gave his last public conference in February 1997 at the age of 91.

He leaves behind a prolific presentation of the truth in the Bible. His major work, *Life-study of the Bible,* comprises over 25,000 pages of commentary on every book of the Bible from the perspective of the believers' enjoyment and experience of God's divine life in Christ through the Holy Spirit. Witness Lee was the chief editor of a new translation of the New Testament into Chinese called the Recovery Version and directed the translation of the same into English. The Recovery Version also appears in a number of other languages. He provided an extensive body of footnotes, outlines, and spiritual cross references. A radio broadcast of his messages can be heard on Christian radio stations in the United States. In 1965 Witness Lee founded Living Stream Ministry, a non-profit corporation, located in Anaheim, California, which officially presents his and Watchman Nee's ministry.

Witness Lee's ministry emphasizes the experience of Christ as life and the practical oneness of the believers as the Body of Christ. Stressing the importance of attending to both these matters, he led the churches under his care to grow in Christian life and function. He was unbending in his conviction that God's goal is not narrow sectarianism but the Body of Christ. In time, believers began to meet simply as the church in their localities in response to this conviction. In recent years a number of new churches have been raised up in Russia and in many eastern European countries.

OTHER BOOKS PUBLISHED BY
Living Stream Ministry

Titles by Witness Lee:

Abraham—Called by God	0-7363-0359-6
The Experience of Life	0-87083-417-7
The Knowledge of Life	0-87083-419-3
The Tree of Life	0-87083-300-6
The Economy of God	0-87083-415-0
The Divine Economy	0-87083-268-9
God's New Testament Economy	0-87083-199-2
The World Situation and God's Move	0-87083-092-9
Christ vs. Religion	0-87083-010-4
The All-inclusive Christ	0-87083-020-1
Gospel Outlines	0-87083-039-2
Character	0-87083-322-7
The Secret of Experiencing Christ	0-87083-227-1
The Life and Way for the Practice of the Church Life	0-87083-785-0
The Basic Revelation in the Holy Scriptures	0-87083-105-4
The Crucial Revelation of Life in the Scriptures	0-87083-372-3
The Spirit with Our Spirit	0-87083-798-2
Christ as the Reality	0-87083-047-3
The Central Line of the Divine Revelation	0-87083-960-8
The Full Knowledge of the Word of God	0-87083-289-1
Watchman Nee—A Seer of the Divine Revelation ...	0-87083-625-0

Titles by Watchman Nee:

How to Study the Bible	0-7363-0407-X
God's Overcomers	0-7363-0433-9
The New Covenant	0-7363-0088-0
The Spiritual Man 3 volumes	0-7363-0269-7
Authority and Submission	0-7363-0185-2
The Overcoming Life	1-57593-817-0
The Glorious Church	0-87083-745-1
The Prayer Ministry of the Church	0-87083-860-1
The Breaking of the Outer Man and the Release ...	1-57593-955-X
The Mystery of Christ	1-57593-954-1
The God of Abraham, Isaac, and Jacob	0-87083-932-2
The Song of Songs	0-87083-872-5
The Gospel of God 2 volumes	1-57593-953-3
The Normal Christian Church Life	0-87083-027-9
The Character of the Lord's Worker	1-57593-322-5
The Normal Christian Faith	0-87083-748-6
Watchman Nee's Testimony	0-87083-051-1

Available at
Christian bookstores, or contact Living Stream Ministry
2431 W. La Palma Ave. • Anaheim, CA 92801
1-800-549-5164 • www.livingstream.com